CLARENDON LIBRARY OF LOGIC AND PHILOSOPHY

General Editor: L. Jonathan Cohen

DIVINE COMMANDS AND MORAL REQUIREMENTS

DIVINE COMMANDS
AND MORAL
REQUIREMENTS

PHILIP L. QUINN

CLARENDON PRESS · OXFORD
1978

Oxford University Press, Walton Street, Oxford OX2 6DP

NEW YORK TORONTO MELBOURNE WELLINGTON
IBADAN NAIROBI DAR ES SALAAM LUSAKA CAPE TOWN
KUALA LUMPUR SINGAPORE JAKARTA HONG KONG TOKYO
DELHI BOMBAY CALCUTTA MADRAS KARACHI

British Library Cataloguing in Publication Data
Quinn, Philip L
  Divine commands and moral requirements. –
  (Clarendon library of logic and philosophy).
  1. Religious ethics   2. God-Will
  I. Title
  171'.1   BJ118   78-40083

  ISBN 0-19-824413-4

*Printed in Great Britain by
Billing & Sons Limited, Guildford, London and Worcester*

Preface

THE view that morality in some way depends, at least in part, upon the will of God is an important theme in the history of philosophy. In recent times this idea has not been taken very seriously by prominent moral philosophers. It is often assumed that the view has been refuted or can be shown to be quite implausible in the light of accepted modern doctrine about morality. Because I believe this assumption to be mistaken, I propose to take a fresh look at this issue. What I wish to ask is whether some version of the claim that human morality depends upon divine commands can be defended against serious and sustained philosophical criticism. I am also interested in finding out whether significantly different versions of divine command theory can be formulated. And, finally, I propose to try to discover whether divine command theories are consistent with or can be grafted on to other recent theories of the logic of some of the moral concepts.

The way I shall proceed to tackle these problems may provide some orientation if outlined briefly. In the first chapter I refute an argument which was constructed to show that human moral autonomy is incompatible with unqualified obedience to divine commands. I then formulate, in the second chapter, what I take to be strong forms of the crucial assumptions—the cores or kernels—of three logically distinct types of divine command theory, and I argue that some of these assumptions can be defended against a battery of philosophical objections. In the third chapter I show how two of the three sets of kernel assumptions can be incorporated into more comprehensive theoretical frameworks which include both theological foundations for a theory of moral value, or axiology, and a basis in divine commands for a theory of moral obligation, or deontology. Next I devote two chapters to establishing connections between divine command conceptions of ethics and recent formal work in the logic of the moral concepts. The fourth chapter comprises a construction of a weak divine command theory of moral requirement and obligation by extending Chisholm's logic of requirement into the theological domain and a defence of the resulting theory against standard philosophical objections. The fifth chapter shows that several of the more intriguing recently invented systems of deontic logic, including some logics of conditional obligation, can be furnished with semantical foundations based on a divine command conception of the truth conditions for ought-statements and thereby demonstrates that each of these logical systems is, as it should be, consistent with a divine command conception of the nature of moral obligation. Finally, in the sixth chapter I illustrate the role divine command conceptions can play in dealing with some philosophical problems about the nature of God; I show how it is possible for God to forgive sins and try to solve Anselm's puzzle about how God could be perfectly just and yet mercifully spare some sinners while justly punishing others.

Perhaps some misunderstanding can be avoided if I strongly emphasize here the limitations of what I propose to do. Except for a few of the points made in the first and last chapters, my arguments are mainly concerned with the conceptual coherence, legitimacy, and fruitfulness of divine command theories. I try to prove that none of the standard philosophical objections to such theories comes anywhere near to a conclusive refutation of all varieties of divine command theory. I also try to exhibit the theoretical fertility of a divine command conception by elaborating in schematic fashion several alternative versions of the logical structure of divine command ethics and by making connections with recent work by others on the logic of the moral concepts. So, if I succeed, I shall have established that philosophers do not know, and do not have conclusive reasons for believing, that all divine command theories are incoherent, false, or barren. I regard it as important to establish this conclusion prior to asking whether there are good philosophical reasons for believing that some version of divine command theory is true.

There are, then, at least two very important questions about theological ethics which I have *not* tried to answer. Are there good positive reasons for believing that a version of divine command theory is true? It seems to me that, if there are philosophical reasons of this sort, they must be reasons which justify a whole cluster of relatively specific theological doctrines about the existence and nature of God and about God's relations to and interactions with creatures. It is obvious that the problem of providing a philosophical justification for such doctrines raises the deepest and hardest puzzles in religious epistemology. And I must confess that I have not discussed this knot of problems because at present I have nothing original to contribute to the literature of religious epistemology. Is some particular theory about what God has commanded especially worthy of belief? As I see it, this question can only be answered on the basis of a thorough acquaintance with the content of many concrete systems of theological ethics. There is, after all, disagreement about exactly what God has commanded not only among the several strands of theistic orthodoxy but also among respectable moralists within each major tradition. Only comparative studies of the details of such alternative conceptions of the contents of God's commands will, I believe, enable a philosopher to pass informed judgement on whether any particular system of theological ethics is more worthy of belief than all its competitors. I do not have the competence to perform such case studies in the requisite detail, and, even if I did, completing the task successfully would require recording the results of many years' labour in several large books.

But the fact that I do not discuss these questions, or others like them, in detail in what follows should not be taken to indicate that I do not see their seriousness and importance. Perhaps such questions have even more practical import than those I have chosen to consider. I see my primary task as providing a theoretical and conceptual background against which they will demand, and may receive, more serious and sustained philosophical attention in the near future than they have in the recent past. And I shall be delighted if my arguments succeed in provoking more philosophers to debate these issues with the care they merit.

An earlier version of most of the material in the first chapter was published in *Religious Studies*; I use this material again with the permission of the editor. Parts of the fourth chapter were the basis of a paper I read at the Eastern Division Meeting of the American Philosophical Association in December 1976. Otherwise, the things I have to say here have not yet been subjected to public scrutiny. The bulk of the research was done while I was on sabbatical leave from Brown University during the academic year 1975/76. My colleague, Roderick M. Chisholm, kindly read the completed manuscript and made some valuable suggestions about how it might be improved. I am indebted to Robert M. Adams for pointing out to me a mistake in an earlier version of the fourth chapter. Wilfrid Sellars and L. Jonathan Cohen made written suggestions which helped me with the final revisions.

I dedicate this book to my sisters, Barbara and Elizabeth.

Contents

I

Divine Commands and
Moral Autonomy

It has become fashionable to try to prove the impossibility of there being a God. Findlay's celebrated ontological disproof has in the past quarter-century given rise to vigorous controversy.[1] More recently James Rachels has offered a moral argument intended to show that there could not be a being worthy of worship.[2] What Rachels attempts to establish is that obedience to divine commands would require giving up the role of an autonomous moral agent. If this were so, it would destroy the prospects for a defensible divine command theory of morality. Obedience to divine commands might still in some sense be required of us, but the requirement could not be a moral one. Thus Rachels presents the divine command theorist with a significant challenge. In this chapter I shall examine the position Rachels is arguing for in some detail. I shall endeavour to show that his argument is unsound and, more interestingly, that the genuine philosophical perplexity which motivates it can be dispelled without too much difficulty.

I

Rachels summarizes his position in the form of the following argument:

(1) If any being is God, he must be a fitting object of worship.
(2) No being could possibly be a fitting object of worship, since worship requires the abandonment of one's role as an autonomous moral agent.

[1] J. N. Findlay, 'Can God's Existence be Disproved?' in *New Essays in Philosophical Theology* (ed. A. Flew and A. MacIntyre), New York: Macmillan (1964.) See discussion in the replies to Findlay by G. E. Hughes and A. C. Rainer in the same volume.
[2] J. Rachels, 'God and Human Attitudes', *Religious Studies* 7, (1971), pp. 325-37.

(3) Therefore, there cannot be any being who is God.[3]

In order to test this argument for validity some uniform interpretation of its English modal auxiliaries in terms of a philosophically well-understood set of modalities must be found. It seems clear that Rachels intends (1) to be read as a proposition of *de dicto* logical or conceptual necessity. He claims that 'it is necessarily true that God (if He exists) is worthy of worship. Any being who is not worthy of worship cannot be God.'[4] Hence, no violence is done to his intentions if we recast the argument in the following canonical form:

(4) Necessarily, if some being is God, then that being is worthy of worship.
(5) It is not possible that some being is worthy of worship.
(6) It is not possible that some being is God.

In the restated argument all the modal operators are to be understood as expressing *de dicto* logical necessity and possibility as explicated in one of the standard systems of alethic modal logic in order to avoid fallacies of equivocation. On this interpretation the argument is valid.[5] Furthermore, on Rachels's view that 'God' is not a proper name but a title,[6] there is no reason to object to (4). The soundness of the argument then hangs, as it should, on whether (5) is true.

Now (5) certainly does not express an obvious modal truth, and so it is incumbent upon Rachels to argue for it. That he accepts this onus is evident from the since-clause in (2) which signals the argument which is the most interesting feature of Rachels's paper. Unfortunately, however, Rachels does not make this argument perfectly clear, and so it must be reconstructed for him. The following valid argument would suffice to establish (5) if it were sound:

(7) It is not possible that some being is worthy of worship and that there are some human moral agents.

---

[3] Ibid., p. 335. The argument (1)–(3) is expressed in Rachels's own woɪds.
[4] Loc. cit.
[5] My strategy is to reconstruct Rachels's arguments so that they turn out to be valid in order to focus my criticism on the truth values of their premises. I have, therefore, checked to be sure that the reconstructed arguments are formally valid at least in the Feys system T and the Lewis systems S_4 and S_5.
[6] Rachels, op. cit., p. 333.

(8) Necessarily, there are some human moral agents.
(5) It is not possible that some being is worthy of worship.

To evaluate the soundness of this argument something more must be said about the concept of moral agency. Rachels's views on this matter place him squarely within what might be called, speaking loosely, the Kantian tradition. He asserts that 'to be a moral agent is to be an autonomous or self-directed agent. . . The virtuous man is therefore identified with the man of integrity, i.e. the man who acts according to precepts which he can, on reflection, conscientiously approve in his own heart.'[7] Let us suppose, for the sake of argument, that this view of human moral agency is correct. Rachels admits that it is controversial and requires a detailed treatment which is beyond the scope of his paper. And there are theists who are so impressed with the corruption of the human conscience consequent upon what they take to be original sin that they would certainly deny that we are virtuous if conscientious in this Kantian fashion. Nevertheless, since some theists would agree that human moral agents are autonomous, we should at least try to find out whether Rachels can create consternation for them.

Unfortunately, on this view (8) seems to be false. Far from always being self-directed agents who act on principles they can conscientiously and reflectively approve, most people in fact act in unprincipled and unreflective ways often enough that they cannot conscientiously approve all of their own conduct in their own hearts. And even if each of us is sometimes a moral agent in the requisite sense, this is a contingent truth and not a necessary one. It would be slightly unfair, however, to challenge what is intended as an *a priori* argument on empirical grounds, and so I propose to resort to the somewhat drastic expedient of stipulating that (8) is a necessary truth about the possibility of human moral agency. A more formal paraphrase of (8) can then be expressed as follows:

(9) Necessarily, it is possible that there are human moral agents.

One must as a consequence of this view accept the conclusion that most of us, much of the time, are not in fact fully fledged moral agents, but this is not, I think, an intolerable perversion

[7] Ibid., p. 334.

of at least some of the evaluative uses of 'moral agent'. And now we can reformulate the argument in a more perspicuous way:

(10) It is not possible both (a) that some being is worthy of worship and also (b) that it is possible that there are some human moral agents.

(9)   Necessarily, it is possible that there are human moral agents.

(5)   It is not possible that some being is worthy of worship.

This argument is also valid, and only the acceptability of (10) remains to be examined. Here we reach what is for Rachels's argument the heart of the matter; however, it also seems to be the heart of darkness.

Why should anyone be tempted to accept (10)? Rachels thinks he has found grounds for accepting it in certain features of the concept of worship. In his view, 'That God is not judged challenged, defied or disobeyed, is at bottom a *truth of logic*; to do any of these things is incompatible with taking him as one to be worshipped.'[8] He also says: 'The point is not merely that it would be imprudent to defy God, since we certainly can't get away with it; rather, there is a stronger, *logical* point involved— namely, that if we recognize any being as God, then we are committed, in virtue of that recognition, to obeying him.'[9] Hence, 'in admitting that a being is worthy of worship we would be recognizing him as having an unqualified claim to our obedience.'[10] We are then faced, according to Rachels, with 'a conflict between the role of worshipper, which by its very nature commits one to total subservience to God, and the role of moral agent, which necessarily involves autonomous decision making'.[11] In other words, there is, roughly speaking, supposed to be a conflict between regarding some being as worthy of worship and being a human moral agent. The view that subservience involves obedience will, of course, be restricted to those who conceive of the object of their worship as a person-like entity capable of commanding. Even so, this conception is common enough among religious people to warrant careful treatment.

But, after all, role-conflict is not logical contradiction, and it is not clear just how the alleged conflict is supposed to enhance

[8] Ibid., p. 333.   [10] Ibid., p. 334.   [9] Ibid., p. 332.   [11] Ibid.

the plausibility of (10). For consider what someone who accepts Rachels's views on the logic of worship would be committed to. He would accept, I suppose, the following argument:

(11) Necessarily, a being is God only if he is worthy of worship.
(12) Necessarily, if a being is God only if he is worthy of worship, then for all human persons p and for all actions a, if God commands p to do a, then p ought to do a.
(13) Necessarily, for all human persons p and for all actions a, if God commands p to do a, then p ought to do a.

This argument is valid with the modal operators taken, as before, to express *de dicto* logical necessity, 'a' and 'p' taken to be variables, and 'ought' in (12) and (13) taken to express a moral 'ought'. Since 'God' is not taken to be a proper name, (11)–(13) should be understood as not implying the existence of God, parallel to our construal of (1) and (4). Hence, (13) does not imply by itself any existential claims about God, or for that matter about human persons or actions, but merely expresses the logical connection between the concept of God and the concept of unqualified obedience. Let us also suppose, for the sake of argument, that (11)–(13) are true. The question which remains is how (13) is supposed to support (10). After all, since (13) is consistent with there being no divine commands, it hardly seems to conflict logically with the autonomy of any moral agent.

Rachels has anticipated an objection of this sort. His response is to claim that 'even if God did not require obedience to detailed commands, the worshipper would still be committed to the abandonment of his role as a moral agent *if* God required it'.[12] It is clear that, if God issues commands, then the worshipper is committed to obeying them; what is not so obvious is just how this is supposed to commit the worshipper to abandoning his role as a moral agent. In order to see whether this latter commitment is involved in worship, let us suppose that God does issue a command:

(14) God commands P to do A.

where 'P' and 'A' are constants substituted for the variables 'p' and 'a'. From (13) and (14) it follows:

[12] Ibid., p. 335.

(15) P ought to do A.

It should be noted that (14) is not a necessary truth but that it does imply the existence of God and at least one person. That (14) does not express a necessary truth should be obvious from the fact that, even if God exists necessarily, it is not necessary that he ever issues any commands. Does the supposition expressed by (14) conflict with the autonomy of any moral agent?

Presumably a moral agent might, on reflection, conclude that (15) was unacceptable. He might assert instead:

(16) It is not the case that P ought to do A.

On the assumption that ought-statements can be incompatible, he would then be driven to denying (15) and, to preserve consistency, to denying either (13) or (14). Since (13) is a necessary truth, his only consistent option would be to deny (14). But denying (14) does not by itself compel him to deny the existence of God, for (14) is an internally complex proposition which can be partially analysed as follows:

(17) There is something which is God and which commands P to do A.

The denial of (17) is equivalent to the following:

(18) Everything is such that either it is not God or it does not command P to do A.

And someone can assert (18) without denying the existence of God by asserting its second disjunct and claiming:

(19) God exists but God does not command P to do A.

In other words, an autonomous human moral agent can admit the existence of God if he is prepared to deny that any putative divine command which is inconsistent with his hard-core reflective moral judgements really is a divine command. He can resolve the supposed role-conflict by allowing that genuine divine commands ought to be obeyed unconditionally but also maintaining that no directive which he does not accept on moral grounds is a genuine divine command. For the following three propositions are logically compatible:

(20) God exists.

(21) God sometimes commands agents to do certain things.

(22) God never commands anything an autonomous and well-informed human moral agent would, on reflection, disapprove.

Hence, since (13) does not entail or otherwise support (10) and because Rachels has give no other reason for accepting (10), it is rational to reject (10). Indeed, (10) seems to be demonstrably false. After all, Rachels would admit, as was noted above, the following claim:

(23) It is possible that some being is worthy of worship and that this being issues no commands and that it is possible that there are human moral agents.

Furthermore, an obvious truth is the following:

(24) That some being is worthy of worship and that this being issues no commands and that it is possible that there are human moral agents entails that some being is worthy of worship.

and, using the logical truth,

(25) (Possibly (p and q) and (p and q entail r)) entail possibly (p and r).

it can be validly inferred that

(26) It is possible that some being is worthy of worship and that it is possible that there are human moral agents.

which is the negation of (10). Therefore, the argument for (6) from (4), (5), (9), and (10) is unsound. Rachels has failed to provide what he promised—a sound 'a priori argument against the existence of God which is based on the conception of God as a fitting object of worship'.[13]

---

[13] Ibid., p. 325.

2

At this point one might suspect that, although Rachels's modal argument fails to show that there could not be anything worthy of worship, it does raise some philosophical questions which have not yet been dealt with adequately. This suspicion seems to me essentially correct, and so I shall press on in the attempt to get at the underlying perplexity which might have led Rachels to construct his argument.

One begins to appreciate what may be troubling Rachels when one asks whether someone who proposes to accept (18) is justified in all cases in asserting the second disjunct and denying the first. At first blush it would seem that theists have a good reason for supposing that God would not, indeed could not, command anything which a well-informed autonomous human moral agent should be unable to accept. After all, Rachels explicitly allows that 'it has been admitted as a necessary truth that God is perfectly good; it follows as a corollary that He would never require us to do anything except what is right'.[14] In other words, Rachels would accept the following claim:

(27) Necessarily, a being is God only if he is perfectly good.

with (27) interpreted in the same way as (11). It seems open to anyone who accepts this claim to argue that, because (27) is true, any command which is not acceptable to a well-informed and autonomous human moral agent could not be a divine command. So theists seem driven logically, for reasons which Rachels acknowledges, to accept the second disjunct of (18) and to deny that wicked commands could come from God.

It comes as a surprise, therefore, to find Rachels contending that this line of argument rests on a misunderstanding of (27). What he offers in support of this contention are the following remarks:

We cannot determine whether some being is God without first checking on whether he is perfectly good; and we cannot decide whether he is perfectly good without knowing (among other things) whether his commands to us are right. Thus our own judgment that some actions are right, and others wrong, is logically prior to our

[14] Ibid., p. 335.

recognition of any being as God. The upshot of this is that we cannot justify the suspension of our own judgment on the grounds that we are deferring to God's commands (which, as a matter of logic, must be right); for if, by our own best judgment, the command is wrong, this gives us good reason to withold the title 'God' from the commander.[15]

Now these remarks may be correct; at any rate we may assume that they are for the sake of the argument. However, we do need to note that the situation being described involves epistemic rather than logical priority. What is puzzling is why Rachels thinks this description of a theistic moral agent's epistemic situation shows up a misunderstanding of (27). Surely theists need only be committed to obeying God's commands because they are morally legitimate themselves; they need not be committed to obeying them simply because they are the decrees of a superior power.[16] What could be more natural, then, than using reflective moral judgements as touchstones for determining which claims to moral authority might plausibly be regarded as divine? Doubtless, many theists do in fact surrender their moral autonomy to human institutions and authorities, but then so do many non-theists. What seems clear is that a theist is not required by logic to suspend his moral judgement in the face of any human authority. Of course, a theist may be committed to the view that if God commands then he should obey, but he may not be able to justify the belief that God has commanded a certain action without first having good moral reasons to think that he ought to do what has been commanded.

Why is Rachels inclined to think that a theist should find this situation unsatisfactory? I suspect that it is because he imagines that a theist who uses his own moral judgements as a basis for deciding whether or not to obey commands cannot be yielding the appropriate sort of unqualified obedience which is owed to a being that is worthy of worship. To put the point crudely: if a human moral agent sits in judgement on God's commands, accepting some and rejecting others, then he is not totally subservient to God.

[15] Ibid., pp. 335–6.
[16] However, it should be noted that some divine command theories have it that God's commands are to be obeyed just because he is supremely powerful.

If this is what Rachels supposes, then it is clear that he has misunderstood the position of a theist who is also an autonomous moral agent. This misunderstanding can be traced, I think, to the failure to make an important distinction between unqualified obedience to a command which is of divine origin and unqualified acceptance of the claim that a command is of divine origin. This distinction can be made clearer by examining the contrast between the following propositions:

(28) If God commands P to do A, then P ought to do A only if conditions C are satisfied.

(29) P ought to assent to the claim that God commands P to do A only if conditions C' are satisfied.

Presumably, since a theist will accept (13) and (27), he will reject (28) for any non-vacuous specification of conditions C. This is what unqualified obedience amounts to. But a theist can accept (29) with rather strong non-vacuous specifications of the epistemic conditions C' which qualify his assent to the claim that a command is of divine origin. Because many theists believe that there are powerful evil spirits trying to deceive them, they ought to, and do, require that particularly stringent epistemic conditions be satisfied before they accept the claim that God has promulgated a certain decree. Frequently such conditions are formulated in terms of coherence with scripture and dogma, but there is no logical reason why coherence with moral judgements about which a theist, on reflection, is very certain should not be included in such conditions. It is not as if the theist is sitting in judgement on commands which are known by him to be of divine origin and qualifying his obedience to God. Rather, he is endeavouring to determine whether certain commands are genuinely God's and, hence, ought to be obeyed and is qualifying his assent to claims of moral authority made on religious grounds. This he must do somehow if he is not to become a fanatic or the victim of charismatic religious charlatans. Therefore, it is a mistake to suppose that a theist who is cautious about accepting putative divine commands as genuine is thereby qualifying his obedience to those commands which he does accept with justification as being of divine origin.[17]

[17] A similar critical point has been elaborated in some detail in R. A. Oakes, 'Reply to Professor Rachels', *Religious Studies* 8 (1972), pp. 165–7.

But, surely, it may be objected in support of Rachels, God might command just anything; since he is necessarily omnipotent, there are no limits on what he could will. In particular, it might seem that he could command a human person to abandon his role as a moral agent, that is to say, to relinquish his moral autonomy. If so, then by instantiation of (13) it would follow:

(30) Necessarily, if God commands P to relinquish his moral autonomy, then P ought to relinquish his moral autonomy.

And if God did so command, it would be correct to assert:

(31) God commands P to relinquish his moral autonomy.

and to infer by *modus ponens*:

(32) P ought to relinquish his moral autonomy.

Surely (32), though not a logical impossibility, seems to be troublesome at least to those theists who wish to subscribe to a Kantian view of moral agency. Except, of course, that such theists would be prepared to maintain:

(33) It is not the case that P ought to relinquish his moral autonomy.

and to infer by *modus tollens*:

(34) It is not the case that God commands P to relinquish his moral autonomy.

One man's *modus ponens* is another's *modus tollens*, and our imagined Kantian theist is at no logical disadvantage in this argument. Indeed, since he accepts (27), he might assert the stronger proposition:

(35) It is not possible that God commands P to relinquish his moral autonomy.

and justify this claim in terms of a theory of the divine attributes which has it that God's power to command is necessarily limited by his perfect goodness.

In any case, we have found no argument so far, *a priori* or empirical, which would pose a logical threat to the position of a theist who wishes to adopt a Kantian view of moral agency.

3

What does seem to threaten the position of our Kantian theist is not a matter of the logic of the concepts of moral agency or of worthiness of worship but rather of certain possible questions of fact and evidence. It seems possible that a theist should have both good reasons for believing that God has commanded him to perform a certain action and good reasons for believing that it would be morally wrong for him to perform that action. Thus a theist can be confronted with moral dilemmas of a peculiar sort. The story of Abraham and Isaac provides a convenient illustration of the kind of moral problem which might arise. This story need not be interpreted in the idiosyncratic Kierkegaardian manner as involving a teleological suspension of the ethical in order for Abraham's dilemma to raise a serious moral problem.[18]

We may imagine that Abraham accepts (13). He also has good reason to accept the following:

(36) God commands Abraham to kill Isaac.

After all, Abraham had reason to believe that God had made and kept some rather remarkable promises to him in the past, such as giving him a son when he was 100 years old.[19] Thus Abraham, we may suppose, had what he took to be good inductive evidence to support his assent to (36). Hence, from (13) and (36) he could infer:

(37) Abraham ought to kill Isaac.

But now we may also imagine, anachronistically perhaps, that Abraham is a Kantian moral agent who is inclined to accept, on reflection, the following argument:

(38) One ought not to kill an innocent child.
(39) Isaac is an innocent child.
(40) Abraham ought not to kill Isaac.

Obviously, Abraham cannot consistently accept both (37) and (40). What is he to do? Well, supposing that he does not even consider doubting (39), he must reject either (36) or (38). But

---

[18] For criticism of the Kierkegaardian interpretation, see G. Outka, 'Religious and Moral Duty: Notes on *Fear and Trembling*' in *Religion and Morality* (ed. G. Outka and J. P. Reeder), Garden City: Doubleday (1973).

[19] Genesis 21: 1–3.

he has good reasons to accept both of these propositions. His reasons for accepting (36), being inductive, are admittedly less than logically conclusive. However, since even reflective moral judgements are fallible, his reasons for accepting (38) will also be logically inconclusive; perhaps his reflective moral judgements are slightly askew.

There is, of course, an easy way out of this dilemma. Kant was aware of it, and it is rather surprising that Rachels does not seem to be. In discussing the case of an inquisitor, Kant makes these remarks:

That it is wrong to deprive a man of his life because of his religious faith is certain, unless (to allow for the most remote possibility) a Divine Will, made known in extraordinary fashion, has ordered it otherwise. But that God has ever uttered this terrible injunction can be asserted only on the basis of historical documents and is never apodictically certain. After all, the revelation has reached the inquisitor only through men and has been interpreted by men, and even did it appear to have come to him from God Himself (like the command delivered to Abraham to slaughter his own son like a sheep) it is at least possible that in this instance a mistake has prevailed. But if this is so, the inquisitor would risk the danger of doing what would be wrong in the highest degree; and in this very act he is behaving unconscientiously. This is the case with respect to all historical and visionary faith; that is, the *possibility* ever remains that an error may be discovered in it. Hence it is unconscientious to follow such a faith with the possibility that perhaps what it commands or permits may be wrong, i.e., with the danger of disobedience to a human duty which is certain in and of itself.[20]

Kant's claim, which is bound to be attractive to many modern philosophers, is that Abraham is or can be certain of (38) but cannot have reasons good enough to warrant accepting (36). Needless to say, this is a very controversial thesis, and one which Abraham and other theists need not accept. For Abraham can reasonably judge that, in cases of conflict of duties, his actual duty is to obey God's commands because obedience to God's

[20] I. Kant, *Religion Within the Limits of Reason Alone* (tr. T. M. Greene and H. H. Hudson), New York: Harper & Row (1960), p. 175. Kant also says: 'That I ought not to kill my good son is certain beyond a shadow of a doubt; that you, as you appear to be, are God, I am not convinced and will never be even if your voice would resound from the (visible) heavens.' This remark from *Der Streit der Facultäten* is cited in G. Outka, op. cit., p. 235.

commands overrides his other *prima facie* duties in such cases. In so judging he would not abandon his role as an autonomous moral agent, for, as Rachels himself admits, 'if we learn that God (i.e. some being that we take to be God) requires us to do a certain action, and we conclude on this account that the action is morally right, then we have *still* made at least one moral judgement of our own, namely that whatever this being requires is morally right'.[21] Furthermore, Abraham might have very good reasons, at least, it seems, in terms of the evidential canons of his own theistic conceptual framework, for believing that God has given him a command. Hence, he might be certain of (36) and dubious about (38).

Now it is fairly clear that this Abraham is no knight of faith; he is a moral rationalist who disagrees with Kant about the probative force of various sorts of evidence. His position is at least logically consistent. Is it utterly irrational? That depends, I suppose, on whether it is possible to have evidence which makes it certain that God has commanded a certain action. This question raises some of the hardest problems of religious epistemology, but, as far as I know, it remains an open question. For I know of no argument which shows:

(41) It is not possible that there is evidence which makes it certain for Abraham that God has commanded Abraham to kill Isaac.

with 'God' here taken to have existential import. Here we seem to reach an impasse at the epistemological chasm which separates theistic from non-theistic assumptions at the basic level.

Of course, Abraham need not be certain of (36) in any very strong sense; Kant is surely correct in thinking that it is possible that Abraham is mistaken. But neither is the duty not to kill an innocent child 'certain in and of itself' as Kant supposes, or at least there seems to be no good reason for a theist to subscribe to this variety of moral dogmatism. In the absence of logically conclusive evidence either way, Abraham can remain reasonable if for him what (36) expresses is epistemically preferable to what (38) expresses. This may seem unlikely given Abraham's

[21] Rachels, op. cit., p. 336.

total evidence, or ours, but it is not impossible. It is not that Abraham need be thought of as acting unconscientiously; he is running grave risks of doing wrong no matter how he acts. As he sees it, if he kills Isaac and God has not commanded it, he acts wrongly, but equally if he does not kill Isaac and God has commanded it, he acts wrongly. His dilemma is an agonizing one, and ordinary theists should breathe a sigh of relief because it does not confront them. However, if a theist like Abraham confronts such a dilemma, then it does seem unfair to accuse him of being unconscientious simply because he must, as he sees it, risk doing wrong and cannot be infallibly certain what would be wrong to do in his circumstances. Soldiers who in time of war have to decide whether to shoot certain people, not knowing whether they are guerrillas armed with grenades or innocent civilians, also run serious moral risks, but even if a soldier kills an innocent civilian he need not be regarded as having acted unconscientiously. Risky moral decisions made under anything short of perfect certainty without possibility of mistake can have appalling consequences even if they are made in reasonable ways.

If our Abraham is neither conceptually confused nor provably irrational, is he wicked? It is not clear that this is the case. Abraham freely accepts the moral principle:

(42) If God commands someone to kill an innocent person, then he ought to kill that person.

Is this principle a manifestly repugnant one? A theist, arguing on his own ground, need not be driven to agree that it is. From a consequentialist point of view he can maintain that God, since he is omniscient, omnipotent, and perfectly good, can appropriately compensate both the killer and his victim in the relevant felicific or beatific respects either here or hereafter. Furthermore, on more formal grounds a theist can successfully apply the universalizability or reciprocity test to (42). He may acknowledge that if God commands someone to kill him then that person ought to kill him, for he may think that he would acquire special merit in the sight of God were he to be a willing sacrifice in such circumstances. He might, of course, consistent with this admission, also believe that no one who claims to have been commanded by God to sacrifice him has in fact been so commanded, and so resist vigorously all sorts of assassination attempts by religious fanatics. The most a theist can be forced to concede, provided he is moderately clever, is that (42) *sounds* harsh and inhumane. But then he will hasten to add that this is merely because we do not understand why God commands what he does, though we may trust that it is all for the best.

If correct, this establishes that our rationalistic Abraham has a way out of the moral dilemma posed by (37) and (40) which does not require him to abandon his role as an autonomous moral agent. Furthermore, this way out allows that he may consistently accept the command to sacrifice Isaac as specifying his actual moral duty and, within his own conceptual framework, correctly claim that he is neither irrational nor wicked. Of course, he may well be mistaken. And, naturally enough, many non-theists, who do not so much as sympathize with the assumptions of this framework, will be scandalized. Such non-theists may, for example, find the compensations and special merits alluded to above utterly fanciful and quite literally incredible. They may claim that if theists can swallow all this then they are dangerous and undesirable people to have around, and may devoutly wish that there should be fewer theists so that the moral order might stand a better chance of being stable and secure. What this shows is the depth of the differences which can separate some theists from some non-theists on practical matters. Perhaps Kant's way out of the dilemma is the only exit a non-theist is prepared to tolerate on the part of a theist. This would show, if it were so, something about the limits of the non-theist's tolerance. It would not establish that the theist has confused or inconsistent beliefs. Nor would it prove, as Rachels appears to believe, that theistic belief is bound to take the worshipper 'beyond morality' or that theistic beliefs should, in this respect, be regarded as a source of 'severe embarrassment'.[22]

4

Perhaps some embarrassment for theism could be generated by means of a more careful scrutiny of some of the central concepts used in the argument so far. The terms 'obedience' and 'autonomy' have been used rather loosely, and artfully

---

[22] Ibid., p. 337.

contrived definitions of these or related terms might lead to a result that would bother the theist. In any case, this possibility seems interesting enough to warrant some further exploration.

Let us consider first the notion of obedience. When would it be appropriate to say that someone is actually obeying a command rather than merely doing what has, as it happens, been commanded? A suggestion as to how this question might be answered is found in the following remarks by Max Weber:

'Obedience' will be taken to mean that the action of the person obeying follows in essentials such a course that the content of the command may be taken to have become the basis of action for its own sake. Furthermore, the fact that it is so taken is referable only to the formal obligation, without regard to the actor's own attitude to the value or lack of value of the content of the command as such.[23]

As it stands, the suggestion is a bit nebulous; moreover, it seems stipulative rather than lexicographically descriptive. However, it does suffice to motivate the introduction of a technical notion of subservience which may be formulated as follows:

(43) Agent p is subservient in doing action a if and only if p's only reason for doing a is p's belief that a has been commanded.

It is clear that (43) does not quite capture the concept which is relevant to the problem at hand. After all, the theist need not be subservient to earthly commanders in anything he does; he may even consider himself obliged by conscience to engage in civil disobedience from time to time. What is wanted is a notion of religious subservience, which can be stated as follows:

(44) Agent p is religiously subservient in doing action a if and only if p's only reason for doing a is p's belief that a has the property of being commanded by God.

'Religious subservience' is, of course, a term of art; however, it may express some of what Rachels has in mind when he speaks of the worshipper's 'total subservience to God'.[24] And even if

---

[23] M. Weber, *The Theory of Social and Economic Organization* (tr. A. M. Henderson and T. Parsons), New York: Free Press (1964), p. 327.

[24] Rachels, op. cit., p. 334.

it is not exactly what Rachels intends, the concept of religious subservience has some interest in its own right.

It is a bit harder to see just how the notion of autonomy should be reshaped to suit present purposes. Since at this point no pretence to either lexicographical accuracy or historical fidelity is being made, misunderstanding will be avoided if technical locutions are introduced to pick out the concepts under discussion. A preliminary stab at what is wanted can be made using the following stipulation:

(45)   Agent p is correct in doing action a if and only if p's only reason for doing a would, if true, suffice to show that a is what p ought to do.

The intuitive idea encapsulated in this stipulation is that an agent acts correctly provided that his reason for action provides conclusive epistemic warrant for the conclusion that he acts as he ought to do. The reason why (45) represents only a preliminary attempt to capture the concept being sought is that a particular agent can be both religiously subservient and correct in doing a particular action. To show that this is the case a theist may deploy the following valid argument:

(46)   Necessarily, if God is perfectly good, then for all actions a and for all agents p, if a has the property of being commanded by God, then a is what p ought to do.
(27)   Necessarily, God is perfectly good.
(47)   Necessarily, for all actions a and for all agents p, if a has the property of being commanded by God, then a is what p ought to do.

Let us suppose, no reason to the contrary being obvious, that this argument is sound. Consider now a particular agent P and a particular action A. Assume that P is religiously subservient in doing A. This implies that P's only reason for doing A is his belief that A has the property of being commanded by God. If this belief were true, we could assert:

(48)   A has the property of being commanded by God.

But (47) and (48) together entail:

(49)   A is what P ought to do.

Hence, P's only reason for doing A would, if true, suffice to show, by a valid and sound deductive argument, that A is what P ought to do, and this implies that P is correct in doing A. Of course, this line of argument involves assuming that (47) is true, but that assumption seems unproblematic because (47) follows from (46), which is innocuous enough, and (27), which even Rachels will allow. Therefore, we must cast about for a concept rather different from correctness if we wish to make trouble for the religiously subservient theist.

The term 'moral correctness' will serve to pick out the required concept. It can be explicated in the following way:

(50) Agent p is morally correct in doing action a if and only if there is some property m such that (i) m makes a what p ought to do, and (ii) p's only reason for doing a is p's belief that a has m.

The idea behind this stipulation is that an agent acts morally correctly provided that his reason for action is the belief that the action in question has a certain property and that the very property he believes the action to have makes it the thing he ought to do. Of course, (50) and (44) are not inconsistent, for the property referred to in (50) might be identical with the property of being commanded by God. Thus, consider again a particular agent P and a particular action A. Suppose both that P's only reason for doing A is P's belief that A has the property of being commanded by God and that being commanded by God makes A what P ought to do. On these suppositions, P is morally correct in doing A, and P is religiously subservient in doing A. But notice that we have, in effect, imported a variant of divine command theory of what ought to be into this argument in assuming that being commanded by God makes A what P ought to do. This assumption would be distasteful to many theists and to almost all non-theistic moralists.

So let us, for the moment, rule out this possibility by means of the following stipulation:

(51) For all agents p, all actions a and all properties m, it is not the case both that m makes a what p ought to do and that m is identical with the property of being commanded by God.

It is easy to see that (44), (50) and (51) are an inconsistent triad. Assuming (51), the proof goes as follows. Consider an arbitrary agent P and an arbitrary action A. Suppose, first, that P is morally correct in doing A. Then, according to (50), some particular M makes A what P ought to do and P's only reason for doing A is his belief that A has M. But then, by (51), M is not identical with the property of being commanded by God. Hence, it is not the case that P's only reason for doing A is his belief that A has the property of being commanded by God. Therefore, by (44), it is not the case that P is religiously subservient in doing A. Suppose, second, that P is religiously subservient in doing A. Then, according to (44), P's only reason for doing A is his belief that A has the property of being commanded by God. By (51), for arbitrary M, either M is not identical with the property of being commanded by God or M does not make A what P ought to do. If M makes A what P ought to do, then, since M is not identical with the property of being commanded by God, it is not the case that P's only reason for doing A is P's belief that A has M, in which case P is not morally correct in doing A by (50). On the other hand, if M is identical with the property of being commanded by God, M does not make A what P ought to do, in which case P is not morally correct in doing A by (50). In either case, P is not morally correct in doing A. Therefore, given (51), (44) and (50) are inconsistent.

What this shows, roughly speaking, is that, on the assumption that a certain version of divine command theory is false, in doing an action A an agent P cannot be both religiously subservient and morally correct in the technical senses given to these notions. It is not surprising that, allowed enough latitude for stipulation, one can introduce incompatible terms into a philosophical vocabulary. The interesting question is whether the theist would, or should, be bothered by such contrivances. But it is not difficult to see that the theist need not be unduly perturbed by this particular set of stipulations. After all, he may simply reject (51).[25] Moreover, even if he chooses not to reject (51), he can challenge (50) by pointing out that it places such stringent conditions on moral correctness that even secular

---

[25] If this is done, some one of the divine command theories we shall discuss later on may then be adopted.

moral theorists may find it embarrassing. Notice that (50) requires that an agent's only reason for doing an action that is morally correct be his belief that it has the very property which, as it happens, makes that action what he ought to do. But consider two agents P_1, a utilitarian, and P_2, deontologist, and two actions A_1 and A_2 which are alike in all morally relevant respects. Suppose that P_1 does A_1 because he believes that A_1 has the property of maximizing expected utility and that P_2 does A_2 because he believes that A_2 has the property of being prescribed by a correct moral rule. On the assumption that both these properties do not make an action what one ought to do, at least one of these agents, and possibly both, are not morally correct in doing what they do. But this would seem to be too harsh a judgement. Since most, perhaps all, human agents frequently do what they ought to do for mixed reasons or the wrong reasons, when indeed they even manage to do what they ought to do, it would seem that (50) stipulates an unreasonably high standard for moral correctness in action. Perhaps it is a symptom of unhealthy scrupulosity when an agent is much concerned with moral correctness in the sense of (50); an agent might well do what he ought to do more often and with less strain, and lead a happier life to boot, if he aspired only to correctness in action in the sense of (45) and, in addition, took reasonable precautions to include many truths and few falsehoods among his reasons for action. If endorsing (50), or something like it, is the price that must be paid to bother the theist, then moral theorists may be unwilling to pay such a high price for such meagre benefits, particularly since a theist can avoid this particular spot of bother by the simple expedient of abandoning (51) and endorsing a divine command theory of what makes actions obligatory. And, even if some non-theists are willing to accept (50), there seems to be no compelling reason why a theist should accept it.

I shall conclude this chapter with a summary of the argument against Rachels. In the first section I tried to show that Rachels's attempt to prove that no being could be a fitting object of worship rests on a false premise and is, therefore, unsound. In the next section I contended that two other arguments, which can be constructed from premisses congenial to Rachels in order to embarrass a theist who would hold a Kantian view of moral agency, turn out on close inspection to be inconclusive or to rest on confusions. In the third section I attempted to elucidate how a theist might consistently deal with conflicts between divine commands and ordinary moral duties so as to make sense of the story of Abraham and Isaac without retreating to Kierkegaardian irrationalism. And in the last section I have tried to show how with a bit of ingenuity one can construct contextually incompatible definitions of religious subservience and moral correctness, but I have argued that there is no reason for a theist to be especially perturbed by such artifices. I have not undertaken to show that the views I atrtibute to theists are plausible given the collection of evidential beliefs I share with Rachels; I suspect I could not hope to succeed at that task. Instead, I have merely tried to defend theistic views against some arguments which purport to demonstrate that they could not possibly be true. In addition, I have tried to set the stage for a closer look at the view, held by some audacious theists, that human morality depends upon the commands of God. Subsequently, we shall be examining several versions of that philosophical position.

II

In Defence of the
Divine Command Conception

THROUGH the ages people have worried about the relations between religion and morality. At one time it was widely feared that decent morals could not long survive a decline in religious belief, but the example of eminent Victorians shows that moral earnestness can go hand in hand with an absence of religious commitment. Today the pendulum of opinion seems to have swung in the other direction; many people are inclined to believe that morality is in every respect independent of religion. Most modern philosophers subscribe to some version of the thesis that morality is autonomous. Such philosophers emphatically reject the claim that what is ethically right or wrong depends upon the command or choice of God. It is often said that divine command theories of ethics are preposterous or obviously untenable.

It is, however, one thing to reject a claim and quite another to refute it. Perhaps if we inspect some divine command theories carefully, it will not turn out to be so obvious that they are untenable; it may even be that there are some defensible theories of this sort. In this chapter I shall challenge what I take to be the conventional wisdom about these matters. I shall argue that philosophers have not succeeded in refuting certain divine command theories, and, therefore, are not justified in rejecting them. My argument divides naturally into three stages. First I shall explain what I take a divine command theory of ethics to be and what consequences I suppose such a theory should have. Next I shall formulate with some care the central assertions of three distant divine command theories, suggest how other theories of the same sorts could be formulated and explore some of the consequences of these theories. Finally I shall consider a number of objections to such theories and try to show that none of them serves to refute all of the theories under discussion. The upshot of the argument, if it succeeds, will be to place the burden of proof squarely on the shoulders of the opponents of divine command theories, which is where, in my opinion, if continues to belong.

I

I.1 *Terminological Matters.* Since the theories we shall consider deal with what God commands, we should at the outset be as clear as we can be about how we propose to use the term 'God'. That term, as orthodox theists use it, is supposed to designate a person-like entity which actually is very powerful, wise, and good. What is not so clear about orthodox usage is what the term is supposed to designate in various possible worlds other than the actual world. On the one hand, we might think of 'God' as a title rather like 'Caesar'.[1] Though Antony was never Caesar, he might have been; and Nero was Caesar though he might not have been. Presumably an individual has a title in virtue of possessing certain properties. An individual which possesses the requisite properties in one possible world may lack them in another. Thus, it might turn out that Yahweh is God in the actual world but Baal is God in some other possible world. On the other hand, we might think of 'God' as a proper name rather like 'Socrates'. Though Socrates might have been foolish, he was in fact wise; and Socrates was a good man though he might not have been. Presumably an individual can exemplify different properties in different possible worlds. Thus, it may be that God commands Abraham to kill Isaac in the actual world but does not do so in some other possible world.

There is a case in which the titular and nominal uses of 'God' coalesce. Suppose all the properties whose possession is requisite for bearing the title 'God' are also essential properties of the individual named 'God'. Since an essential property is

---

[1] The idea that 'God' functions as a title is discussed in Nelson Pike, 'Omnipotence and God's Ability to Sin', *American Philosophical Quarterly* 6 (1969), pp. 208–16.

one an individual possesses in every possible world where it exists, the individual named 'God' will have the title 'God' in every world where it exists. This supposition, however, would not be easy to defend in the absence of some strong and controversial assumptions about the divine nature, and so it would be better to make the argument without it if possible. It will suffice for our purposes, I think, to make two weaker assumptions. First, the term 'God' functions like a proper name in that it picks out the same individual in all possible worlds where it picks out any individual, regardless of how that individual may alter from world to world. And, second, at least some of the things commanded by God differ as possible worlds vary. In brief, we shall assume that the individual named 'God' and believed by theists to be actually wise, powerful, and good, if there is such an individual, does not command exactly the same things in every world where he exists.

God, we may suppose, could command all sorts of things. He could command that the Red Sea parts for Moses or that the sun stands still over Jericho. From the point of view of ethical theory, the kinds of commands of interest will be commands directed to human agents concerning the performance of actions. Thus, God might command that Moses leads the Israelites toward the Promised Land or that all people honour their parents. Such commands can be schematically represented as having propositional objects expressed by sentences whose general form is 'S does A'. However, because we shall not be concerned with the internal logical structure of sentences having this form, it will prove to be simpler to symbolize the propositional objects of such commands with the usual propositional variables. Thus, one of the basic locutions of the theories we shall consider will have the form 'God commands that p'. We shall not discuss the ways in which God might promulgate his commands. God might, for all I know, inspire the writers of Scripture, speak out of a burning bush, make the Pope infallible, or do any one of a number of other things to communicate his commands to human beings. Nor shall we stop to consider the epistemological problems involved in coming to know that a religious prescription is a genuine divine command. We shall only consider some of the relations which might obtain between divine commands and ethical status.

But the slightest reflection on ethical discourse reveals a bewildering variety. Distinctions are made between good and bad, right and wrong, obligatory and supererogatory; agents, their motives, their actions and the consequences of these actions are subjected to ethical evaluation. Philosophers differ on the question of how all these matters would be properly unified in a comprehensive and adequate moral theory. Doubtless a complete divine command theory would turn out to be a very complicated and intricate construction. However, the kernel of a divine command theory can, I believe, be formulated using only three basic concepts; they are the notions of ethical requirement, ethical permission and ethical prohibition. It will be convenient to express these concepts using sentential operators, which map sentences into sentences. Thus the three fundamental locutions of our theories will have the form: 'It is required that p', 'It is permitted that p' and 'It is forbidden that p'. Some philosophers who write about the logic of requirement take as their fundamental locution a two-place predicate of the form 's_1 when it obtains requires s_2' which is supposed to express a relation defined on ordered pairs of states of affairs.[2] This refinement facilitates discussion of some interesting issues having to do with conditional requirement and is, therefore, a step in the direction of greater realism. But complexity is the price of realism in this case, and for our purposes this complexity would be a distraction not worth the price. The simpler locutions will, in the present context, illuminate without distorting what I take to be the important features of divine command theories.

A divine command theory will assert some connections or relations between things which can be expressed in our ethical vocabulary and things which can be expressed in our theological vocabulary. Obviously not just any sentence which contains locutions of both sorts will count as part of a divine command theory. And so we need to get clear about the logical shape a divine command theory should have and about what its consequences should be.

---

[2] An example is Roderick M. Chisholm, 'Practical Reason and the Logic of Requirement', *Practical Reason* (ed. Stephan Körner), Oxford: Basil Blackwell (1974), pp. 1–17.

I.2   *Theoretical Constraints.* When we specify conditions which a theory must satisfy if it is to count as a divine command theory, it would seem to be sound policy, at least initially, to introduce only minimal constraints. If this policy is adopted, several divine command theories can be generated, as we shall see below. Which of the alternatives someone prefers to defend, or ought to wish to defend, then becomes an interesting problem which raises some hard questions about plausibility.

A few rather weak necessary conditions for being a divine command theory come immediately to mind. Surely a divine command theory ought to be subject to the following constraints:

(C1) Necessarily, for all p, if it is required that p, then God commands that p.

(C2) Necessarily, for all p, if it is forbidden that p, then God commands that not-p.

Moreover, a divine command theory ought to preserve at least some of the usual logical relations among requirement, permission and prohibition. Two rather obvious principles which ought to govern our theory construction are, therefore, the following:

(C3) Necessarily, there is no p such that it is permitted that p and it is forbidden that p.

(C4) Necessarily, there is no p such that it is required that p and it is not permitted that p and it is not forbidden that p.

All the theories we shall consider will be constructed in such a way that (C1)–(C4) are satisfied.

At this point it would be well to deal briefly with a philosophical puzzle. Kierkegaard is the author of *Fear and Trembling.* Suppose it is required that Kierkegaard remains celibate. According to (C1), God commands that Kierkegaard remains celibate. But, if we understand our assertions about requirements to make *de re* attributions, as seems natural, our supposition leads us to say that it is also required that the author of *Fear and Trembling* remains celibate. Then, according to (C1), God also commands that the author of *Fear and Trembling* remains celibate. This seems, to say the least, a bit incongruous with our ordinary use of sentences about commands. If Colonel Sanders commands that Private Schweik guards the secret plans and Private Schweik is the chubbiest Czech spy, it does not follow that Colonel Sanders has commanded that the chubbiest Czech spy guards the secret plans. But are we to imagine that God issues as many commands as there are true descriptions of Kierkegaard when he commands that Kierkegaard remains celibate? If so, God's commanding is a strange activity indeed.

We might, I think, deal with the puzzle in a simple way by insisting that assertions about divine commands, unlike many ordinary assertions about human commands, are always to be understood as making *de re* attributions. This stipulation would simplify the formulation of our theories without contradicting any well-established theological or philosophical dogma. Alternatively, we might achieve the same result as regards our puzzle by defining a technical sense of divine commanding in the following manner:

(D) God commands that p = Df For some q, God orders that it be the case that q and, for some r, (i) it is the case that r; (ii) the proposition that r&q entails the proposition that p; and (iii) the proposition that r&p entails the proposition that q.

As far as I can tell, either way we choose to proceed in dealing with this puzzle will suffice for our present purposes.

But (C1)–(C4) do not suffice to differentiate divine command theories from other theological perspectives on ethics. After all, even an opponent of a divine command theory might concede that God commands something if it is required and go on to say that it is precisely because a thing is required that God commands it. We should, therefore, continue to cast about until we discover some propositions which divine command theorists would affirm and others would deny.

In the course of this search we would do well to remember that a divine command theorist *need not* disagree with the conventional moral wisdom about what actually has been, is and will be required, permitted, or forbidden, though he *may* in fact dissent from common moral views. The discrepancies of theoretical importance emerge, rather, when attention is focused on allegedly hypothetical situations. Some examples will help to clarify this point. Consider some type of action which almost everyone would allow to be morally forbidden, for instance, torturing young children for one's own pleasure. A divine command theorist might assert that God commands that Smith does not torture young children for his own pleasure. But he might also claim something like this:

If God were to command that Smith tortures young children for his own pleasure, then it would be required that Smith tortures young children for his own pleasure.

Or think of some sort of action which would be widely regarded as morally required, for example, keeping one's promises. A divine command theorist might admit that God does command this and yet maintain something like the following:

If God were to command that Jones does not keep his promises, then it would be forbidden that Jones keeps his promises.

Again, there would be general agreement that it is permitted but not required that Brown plays golf on Wednesdays, and permitted and not forbidden that Harris eats chocolate ice cream. Yet a divine command theorist would wish to assert things like

If God were to command that Brown plays golf on Wednesdays, then it would be required that Brown plays golf on Wednesdays.

and

If God were to command that Harris does not eat chocolate ice cream, then it would be forbidden that Harris eats chocolate ice cream.

Nor need the examples be fanciful or harmlessly hypothetical. A divine command theorist might claim:

If God were to command that everyone refrains from performing abortions, then it would be required that everyone refrains from performing abortions.

And then such a theorist might go on to add that this is in fact required since God has actually so commanded. Some Christians, I suppose, do hold such views. Or, to take another example, a divine command theorist might make the following claim:

If God were to command that no one eats meat, then it would be forbidden that anyone eats meat.

Clearly some theists do maintain that eating meat is forbidden just because God has commanded that it not be eaten.

In addition to innumerable particular claims like these, a divine command theorist might wish to have certain more general principles turn out to be consequences of his theory. One of them we might call 'Karamazov's Thesis':

If God did not exist, then everything would be permitted.

This thesis certainly asserts a strong dependency of moral status on the nature of things theological, but according to some of the theories we shall discuss Karamazov's Thesis is a theorem.

But perhaps enough has now been said about what we should expect from a divine command theory. If so, we can now turn our attention to formulating theories which satisfy these expectations.

2

II. 1   *The Simple Theory.* In formulating our theories we shall have occasion to make use of some symbolic abbreviations. Let 'Rp' abbreviate 'It is required that p', 'Pp' abbreviate 'It is permitted that p' and 'Fp' abbreviate 'It is forbidden that p'. Further let 'Cp' abbreviate 'God commands that p' and 'Np' abbreviate 'It is necessary that p'. The kernel of the most elementary sort of divine command theory consists of the following claims, each of which is accompanied by its symbolic transcription:

(T1a) It is necessary that, for all p, it is required that p if and only if God commands that p.
$$N(\forall p(Rp \equiv Cp)).$$
(T1b) It is necessary that, for all p, it is permitted that p if and only if it is not the case that God commands that not-p.
$$N(\forall p(Pp \equiv {\sim}C{\sim}p)).$$
(T1c) It is necessary that, for all p, it is forbidden that p if and only if God commands that not-p.
$$N(\forall p(Fp \equiv C{\sim}p)).$$

It is fairly easy to show that T1 satisfies the constraints we wish to impose on divine command theories. For instance, (C1) and (C2) are immediate consequences of (T1a) and (T1c), respectively. According to the law of non-contradiction, God does not both command that p and not command that p in a single possible world, and so (C3) follows from (T1b) and (T1c). Moreover, if we assume the law of excluded middle, (C4) also follows from (T1b) and (T1c). In brief, according to our first theory, the categories of the permitted and the forbidden are both mutually exclusive and collectively exhaustive in each possible world. If God does not exist, then God commands nothing; hence, in that case, for all p, it is permitted that p, and the Karamazov Thesis is a theorem.

What God can command may be a function of what his essential properties are. Thus, if he is necessarily perfectly good, there may be certain things that he commands in no possible world. However, we shall ignore this complication and suppose instead that God is free to command anything he chooses to command. Given this assumption, we can see how our theory accounts for hypothetical examples of the sort presented above. In any possible world where God commands Smith to torture young children, since (T1a) tells us that Smith is required to torture young children there, the material conditional asserting the relation between being commanded to torture and being required to torture will be true. Thus, the presumably counterfactual conditional asserting that if God were to command that Smith tortures children then it would be required that Smith tortures children will be true in the actual world. In other words, if God did command gratuitous cruelty of any one of us or of all of us, then according to (T1a) such behaviour would be required of those so commanded. Similarly, if God were to command that Jones does not keep his promises, then by (T1c) it would be forbidden that Jones keeps his promises. Or, if God were not to command that Jones keeps his promises, then by (T1b) it would be permitted that Jones does not keep his promises. And, of course, if God has, as it happens, commanded that everyone refrains from performing abortions, then according to the theory it is required that everyone refrains from performing abortions. By the same token, if God has commanded that no one eats meat, then eating meat is forbidden to us all.

It is worth stressing that T1, and the other theories we shall be examining later on, can be extended in numerous ways. For instance, we might wish to add to T1, a principle about those things concerning which divine commands remain silent. We can get a terminological hint about how this category might be christened from Locke's remark that '*licitum* is what is not forbidden or commanded by the laws of the society. *Indifferens* what is so by all the other laws'.[3] Using the expression 'Ip' to stand for 'It is indifferent that p', we can state a principle about indifference as follows:

(T1d) It is necessary that, for all p, it is indifferent that p if and only if it is not the case that God commands that p and it is not the case that God commands that not-p.

$$N(\forall p(Ip \equiv \sim Cp \ \& \ \sim C \sim p)).$$

The indifferent is neither required nor forbidden; it is what is permitted but not required. If God were to command nothing at all, then everything would be indifferent. To call what is neither required nor forbidden 'indifferent' may sound a bit odd, for among those things which are indifferent some may be pleasing to God and others may not be. So, perhaps we could also define the supererogatory as that which is indifferent but pleasing to God. I shall not pursue these matters further here because I do not propose to formulate anything like a complete set of principles for each of the theories we discuss. I shall restrict consideration to (T1a)-(T1c) and their analogues. Suffice it to say that the kernel of a divine command theory is not a complete theory, but additional principles can always be added to the kernel. Having only the kernel of each theory before us will be enough for our comparative and critical purposes.

It does seem, then, that T1 has all the features needed to make it a genuine divine command theory of ethics, or at least of that part of ethics which deals with what is required, permitted or forbidden.

II.2 *Some Complex Theories*. There are, however, related theories with equally impressive credentials. Some theists might wish to claim that ethical status depends upon divine fiat only in so far as the individual named 'God' is an entity of a certain sort. For instance, it might be asserted that God's commands generate requirements, permissions and prohibitions only because he is

---

[3] This remark is from Locke's Journal of 28 June 1681 and is quoted by W. von Leyden in his Introduction to John Locke, *Essays on the Law of Nature* (ed. W. von Leyden), Oxford: The Clarendon Press (1954), p. 68.

our creator. Letting 'GM' abbreviate 'God makes the universe', we can build such a stricture into our theory as follows:

(T2a) It is necessary that, for all p, it is required that p if and only if God makes the universe and God commands that p.
$$N(Vp(Rp \equiv GM \ \& \ Cp)).$$

(T2b) It is necessary that, for all p, it is permitted that p if and only if it is not the case that God makes the universe and that God commands that not-p.
$$N(Vp(Pp \equiv \sim(GM \ \& \ C\sim p))).$$

(T2c) It is necessary that, for all p, it is forbidden that p if and only if God makes the universe and God commands that not-p.
$$N(Vp(Fp \equiv GM \ \& \ C\sim p)).$$

It seems clear that having made the universe is not one of God's essential properties. Since, according to common theistic belief, God could have refrained from creating anything, he exists in possible worlds whose other contingent denizens were not made by him. Hence, our new theory T2 asserts something distinct from what T1 asserted. There are, it should be noted, other theories which have the same logical structure as T2 and differ from it only in virtue of favouring some other alleged divine attribute. Thus, some theists might suppose that having power enough to enforce his commands or to see to it that dire consequences ensue if they are disobeyed is the property which insures that God's commands generate ethical status. Others might fix upon loving his human creatures as the relevant property. Since various conjunctions of the properties mentioned, as well as of properties unmentioned, might be built into a theory of this sort, our T2 stands proxy for a whole family of theories.

T2 obviously satisfies the constraints we have imposed on divine command theories. Clearly, (C1) follows from (T2a), and (C2) follows from (T2c). Assuming standard logic, a consequence of (T2b) and (T2c) is that the permitted and the forbidden are mutually exclusive and collectively exhaustive categories in any possible world. Hence, everything is either permitted or forbidden in each possible world, but nothing is both permitted and forbidden in a possible world; and thus both (C3) and (C4) are true. Again we obtain the Karamazov Thesis as a theorem, for if there is no God everything is permitted. But from T2 we also obtain stronger results of the same kind. If God exists but did not make the universe, then nothing is required, nothing is forbidden and everything is permitted. And similar results will hold in other theories belonging to the same family. For instance, if God lacks the power to enforce and punish or fails to love his human creatures, then according to the relevant theories of this family everything is permitted.

The subjunctive and counterfactual conditionals underwritten by T2 and its ilk are a bit more complicated than those supported by T1. In any possible world where God makes the universe and commands Smith to torture young children it is required that Smith tortures young children. Thus the supposedly counter-factual claim that if God were to make the universe and were to command that Smith tortures young children is true, according to the theory, in the actual world. Similarly, if God were to make the universe and were to command Jones not to keep his promises (or were not to command Jones to keep his promises), then Jones would be forbidden to keep his promises (or would be permitted not to keep his promises). And if God has made the universe and has commanded that no one perform abortions (or eat meat), then abortions (or meat-eating) are forbidden. Similar consequences are obtained from other theories of the same family which emphasize divine power or love rather than divine creativity.

It would seem that T2, and other theories of the same type, have the qualifications needed to be properly regarded as divine command theories of the fragment of ethics upon which our attention is focused.

II.3 *Other Complex Theories.* Once we are aware of complex divine command theories like those discussed in the previous section, others with a slightly different logical structure suggest themselves to us. We can formulate a representative theory of this family as follows:

(T3a) It is necessary that, for all p, it is required that p if and only if God makes the universe and God commands that p.

$$N(Vp\ (Rp \equiv GM\ \&\ Cp)).$$

(T3b) It is necessary that, for all p, it is permitted that p if and only if God makes the universe and it is not the case that God commands that not-p.

$$N(Vp(Pp \equiv GM\ \&\ \sim C\sim p)).$$

(T3c) It is necessary that, for all p, it is forbidden that p if and only if God makes the universe and God commands that not-p.

$$N(Vp(Fp \equiv GM \ \& \ C{\sim}p)).$$

T3 is like T2 in being a representative member of a family of theories. Other theories like T3 could be constructed by substituting in place of 'God makes the universe' something like 'God is able to enforce his laws.'

Since T3 does not differ from T2 in what it says about what is required and what is forbidden, (C1) and (C2) follow from (T3a) and (T3c) as before. However, because (T3b) differs from (T2b), a complication arises when we consider (C3) and (C4). We can get at it by noting that in those possible worlds where God does not make the universe nothing is required, nothing is forbidden, and nothing is permitted. Since there is nothing which God both does and does not command in a single possible world, the permitted and the forbidden are mutually exclusive in each possible world and (C3) holds. In each possible world, whatever is forbidden is not permitted and whatever is permitted is not forbidden. But if something is not permitted, it may either be forbidden or fall into none of our three ethical categories, and if something is not forbidden, it may either be permitted or fall into none of our categories. The permitted and the forbidden are not collectively exhaustive in every possible world. However, if something is required, then God has made the universe. On that assumption, what is required is either permitted if God does not command its negation or forbidden if he does. Hence, (C4) also holds in T3. In T3 the Karamazov Thesis is not a theorem, but an equally striking result can be obtained. If there is no God, nothing is required, nothing is permitted and nothing is forbidden. A world of this sort would not be a wildly permissive world; rather it would be a world without ethics. Still, this possibility illustrates another way in which ethical status can depend upon divine commands.

The conditionals supported by T3 are like those supported by T2. In any possible world where God makes the universe and commands torturing young children such torture is required; hence, in the actual world if God were to make the universe and were to command that Smith tortures young children it would be required that Smith torture young children. If God, who made the universe, were to command that promises not be kept (or were not to command that promises be kept), then it would be forbidden to keep promises (or permitted not to keep them). Finally, if God has made the universe and commanded that abortions not be performed (or meat not be eaten), then performing abortions (or eating meat) is forbidden. And, naturally, similar theories with divine power or love replacing divine creativity will have similar consequences.

So there is another family of theories, T3 and its kin, which qualify as divine command theories of requirement, permission, and prohibition.

II.4 *Comparisons of the Theories*. Our somewhat fine-grained analysis of what comprises the kernel of a divine command theory of ethics has shown that there are many theories of this kind. Doubtless someone with a bit of ingenuity could construct others, for it has not been my intention to compile a complete list of such theories. Given this bewildering variety of theories, we should ask ourselves which one among them particular theists hold. Unfortunately, we are seldom provided with enough information to figure out an answer to this question.

To be sure, William of Ockham is often interpreted as having held that those acts we call 'theft', 'adultery', and 'hatred of God' would have been obligatory if God had commanded them.[4] So perhaps Ockham held, or should have held, (T1a) or some consequence of it. But perhaps Ockham intended to use 'God' in such a way that no individual could properly be called 'God' unless he were the creator of the universe, and if he did have in mind this titular use (T2a) or (T3a) would come closer to expressing what he meant. Among contemporary philosophers who talk about divine command theories I have only discovered one who is fairly explicit about which theory he proposes to consider. Robert M. Adams says:

I could say that by 'X is ethically wrong' I mean 'X is contrary to the commands of a *loving* God' (i.e., 'There is a *loving* God and X is contrary to His commands') and by 'X is ethically permitted' I mean 'X is in accord with the commands of a *loving* God' (i.e., 'There is a *loving* God and X is not contrary to His commands').[5]

[4] This is a plausible reading of the famous passage from Ockham's *Super 4 Libros Sententiarum*, II, 19.

[5] Robert M. Adams, 'A Modified Divine Command Theory of Ethical Wrong-

I take this passage to enunciate principles much like (T3b) and (T3c), with 'God makes the universe' replaced by 'God is loving.' Hence, I suppose Adams is discussing at least part of a theory which belongs to the family of T3. Since he says nothing explicit about ethical requirement, I am not sure whether he would accept a relative of (T3a) as a part of the theory he wishes to discuss.

However, it is less important, for our purposes at any rate, to speculate about what various philosophers and theologians have held than to be clear about how the several divine command theories differ among themselves. It bears repeating that divine command theorists are not forced by the logic of their theories to disagree among themselves, or to differ from secular moralists, about what is actually required, permitted, and forbidden. Such differences as there are on this score could arise even among moralists all of whom rejected divine command theories. Where the differences between divine command theorists and others, both theists and non-theists, show up is in their theoretical commitments concerning hypothetical situations and possible worlds other than the actual world. Some of the most salient differences are worth emphasizing. According to T1, in possible worlds where God does not exist, if any, or issues no commands, everything is permitted. In worlds where God commands certain things what is required and forbidden varies from world to world as God's commands do. According to T2, in possible worlds where God does not exist, if any, or God does not make the universe or God issues no commands, everything is permitted. Strikingly, if God did not make the universe, then everything is permitted no matter what he commands, and, moreover, in that case nothing is required or forbidden. Only in worlds where God made the universe and issues some commands is anything required or forbidden, and in those worlds what is required and what is forbidden varies as God's commands do. According to T3, in possible worlds where God did not make the universe nothing is required, nothing is forbidden and nothing is permitted, and obviously the case is the same in worlds, if any, where God does not exist. In worlds

ness', *Religion and Morality* (ed. Gene Outka and John P. Reeder, Jr.), Garden City: Double lay (1973), p. 323.

where God exists and made the universe but issues no commands, everything is permitted. Things are required or forbidden only in worlds where God made the universe and commands certain things, and what is required or forbidden in these worlds varies as God's commands vary.

I cannot say which of these theories a theist ought to prefer, for I know of nothing definitive in theistic traditions which specifies how morals are supposed to alter as possible worlds are varied. Nor am I able to say which theory I find most plausible on independent grounds, for I have no firm intuitions about what is required, permitted, and forbidden in various non-actual possible worlds.

It is, however, worth noting that none of the divine command theories considered presents an easy solution to a puzzle inherent in orthodox Judaeo-Christian moral traditions. The puzzle arises because there is no contradiction in assuming that God commands that p and God commands that not-p, and it can be illustrated by reference to the strange case of Abraham and Isaac. We may suppose, I am sure, that according to orthodox lore God actually did make the universe. He is authoritatively stated to have created the heaven and the earth.[6] Included in the decalogue is a prohibition on killing that comes from God, and so we may also suppose, I think, that God commands that Abraham does not kill Isaac. This seems to be a clear case of a correct specification of the decalogue's injunction. Given these assumptions, all three of our theories tell us that it is forbidden that Abraham kills Isaac and it is required that Abraham does not kill Isaac. But we are also told that God commands that Abraham kills Isaac.[7] Retaining the same assumptions, our theories tell us that it is required that Abraham kills Isaac and it is forbidden that Abraham does not kill Isaac. From all of this it follows, according to our theories, it is not permitted that Abraham kills Isaac but, equally, that it is not permitted that Abraham does not kill Isaac. What is poor Abraham to do? Divine command theories, it seems are not appreciably better than others at answering this question when all the pieces of the puzzle are taken seriously and literally.[8]

---

[6] Genesis 1.   [7] Genesis 22.

[8] I do not wish to claim that orthodox theists are forced to interpret Scripture in this literal way, but some theists, most notably Kierkegaard, have taken this story to illustrate a practical problem which might confront them. The interesting point is that a variant of the problem arises even in divine command theories.

3

If formulating divine command theories is to be more than a pedantic exercise, something must be said about their credibility. Many people, perhaps the majority of our contemporaries, would say that such theories are indefensible. Since this is the case, the burden of proof lies with someone who proposes to defend such theories. It would, of course, be impossible to defend any theory against all conceivable objections or to demonstrate that no objection will ultimately defeat it. After all, it is unlikely that all the interesting objections to any moderately complicated theory have yet been formulated or invented. But a more modest task seems feasible. One can try to defend a theory against all the objections that are common currency at a given time. This is what I shall endeavour to do for divine command theories. I shall try to show that none of the objections usually urged against divine command theories by philosophers are completely persuasive. If I succeed, then divine command theories should no longer be viewed as mere historical curiosities. Rather they should be taken seriously, and arguments for and against them studied with care. I shall proceed in good scholastic fashion by stating a number of objections to such theories and replying to each in turn. Since ten is a nice round number, I propose to discuss ten objections.

III.1   *The Objection from Meaning.* The first objection to be considered can be most readily understood when cast in the form of an argument. The argument goes as follows: (a) A divine command theory is a theory about the meanings of certain ethical terms; (b) Hence, the principles of a divine command theory should express logical equivalences which are also truths of meaning; (c) But the principles proposed in your theories, T1–T3, are obviously not truths of meaning; (d) Therefore, your theories are not divine command theories at all. In order to show that the premiss expressed by (c) is true our objector can call upon a variant of the open-question argument. Suppose, for instance, that 'It is required that people tell the truth' meant 'God commands that people tell the truth' or, more generally, that 's is required' meant 's is commanded by God'. Then it would be silly to ask whether what is commanded by God is required since the claim that what is commanded by

God is required amounts to no more than the assertion that what is commanded by God is commanded by God.

Because there are philosophical problems and confusions aplenty in the domain of theory of meaning, it is not obvious how to reply to this objection. It does, however, seem clear that the logical equivalences expressed by our theories cannot be propositional identities. A plausible criterion for propositional identity is the following: The proposition that p is identical with the proposition that q if and only if, necessarily, for all S, S believes that p if and only if S believes that q.[9] But surely it is possible that someone believes that kindness is morally required without also believing that kindness is commanded by God. Many atheists are, no doubt, in this situation. And it is, quite obviously, also possible for someone to believe that eating fish on Friday is commanded by God without believing that such a diet is morally required. So, if identity of meaning is taken to be propositional identity, then there can be no doubt that the principles of our theories do not express identities of meaning. It is also fairly obvious that not all logical equivalences express truths of meaning. Consider, for example, this truth drawn from Euclidean plane geometry: Necessarily, for all x, x is an equilateral triangle if and only if x is an equiangular triangle. Surely the predicates 'is an equilateral triangle' and 'is an equiangular triangle' are not synonymous, and thus our geometrical truth is not plausibly regarded as a truth of meaning. Indeed, since all necessary truths are, in standard systems of modal logic, logically equivalent, the relation of logical equivalence seems poorly suited to express a sufficient condition for sameness of meaning.

However, we can defeat the objection without having a complete theory of meaning in hand. All we need do is deny the first premiss of the argument. Our divine command theories, T1–T3, are not theories about the meanings of certain ethical terms, and so the logical equivalences they contain are not intended to be truths of meaning. To be sure, some people who have discussed divine command theories have supposed their principles to embody 'definitions' of the ingredient ethical terms, but it seems more sensible to say that the principles of

---

[9] This is a simplified version of a criterion proposed by Roderick M. Chisholm in 'Events and Propositions', *Nous* 4 (1970), pp. 15–24.

any one of our theories are, if true, not true by definition. Someone who accepts a divine command theory may, of course, speak and think in such a way that when he asserts that something is required he intends also to be asserting that the thing in question is commanded by God. Perhaps this is the way some theists do in fact speak and think.[10] Since it is difficult if not impossible always to distinguish those facets of usage which reflect meaning and thus should receive semantic explication from those which reflect entrenched belief and thus should receive pragmatic explication, there is a sense in which a divine command theory can express part of what such a theist means when he engages in ethical discourse. Even so, this does not imply that the principles of a divine command theory are to be understood as stipulative definitions or as true in virtue of the standard meanings of the words used in formulating them.

What we learn, then, from this objection is that our divine command theories ought not to be construed as expressing truths of meaning. If the principles of one of them do express truths, this cannot be shown by lexicographical analysis of the usual meanings of the terms used in their formulation.

III.2   *The Objection from Analysis.* It is sometimes imagined that a divine command theory is supposed to provide a philosophical analysis of the ethical terms or concepts contained in it. If this were so, the *analysans* should have what might be called 'conceptual priority' over the *analysandum*. So far as I know, a satisfactory characterization of conceptual priority has never been given, nor, for that matter, has an adequate account of what a philosophical analysis must do to be successful even been elaborated. But the intuitive idea can be illustrated with a simple example.[11] Gettier problems apart, the following sentence might plausibly be offered as an analysis of propositional knowledge:

(A1) S knows that p iff S has a justified, true belief that p.

But it could hardly be maintained that we get a satisfactory analysis of belief from this sentence:

---

[10] It seems that Adams has a view of this sort in mind. See Adams, op. cit., pp. 321, 325, 346.

[11] The example was suggested to me by James Van Cleve.

(A2) S believes that p iff S stands to p in a relation such that S would know that p if p were justified and true.

Presumably (A1) and (A2) do not differ in truth-value or modal status; if either were a necessary truth, both would be. The relevant difference between them is that the concept of belief has conceptual priority over the concept of knowledge so that it would be proper to analyse knowing in terms of believing but improper to analyse believing in terms of knowing. Just what the priority of belief over knowledge consists in would be hard to say. For those philosophers who exercise themselves with this problem, it is, I suppose, relatively unproblematic what belief is, but what knowledge is puzzles them.

Given this somewhat feeble understanding of what is at stake in working out a philosophical analysis, the objection to divine command theories can be put as follows: (a) A divine command theory purports to provide a philsophical analysis of certain ethical terms or concepts; (b) If a divine command theory were able to accomplish this task, its theological concepts would have priority over its ethical concepts; (c) But the concept of a divine command is more problematic than any of the ethical concepts such as requirement, permission, and prohibition which appear in a theory of this sort; (d) Hence, a divine command theory cannot be taken seriously as a philosophical analysis. As was the case with the previous objection, this one can be defeated by denying its first premiss. A divine command theorist need not admit that he is trying to provide anything so esoteric as a philosophical analysis. What he is doing, he may say, is formulating some principles which express metaphysical truths about the relations between God's will and what we are required, permitted, and forbidden to do. Indeed, since the logical equivalences in our theories are symmetric, a waggish divine command theorist might even claim to be providing a philosophical analysis of certain theological concepts, though this claim seems about as implausible as the premiss of the objection.

The most interesting issue raised by the objection is whether we should concede the priority claim made in its third step. No doubt there are some people who find ethical concepts relatively unproblematic but have great difficulty grasping theological notions. Such people may be quite confident that they understand what it is to be required, permitted, and forbidden, and yet profess not to understand what sort of being God might be or how such a thing could issue commands to human beings. They might, for instance, be perplexed by philosophical arguments which challenge the meaningfulness of talk about God or be worried about whether anything could be omnipotent. In the conceptual schemes of such people ethical notions do have priority over theological notions. But there are, or so I am inclined to suppose, other people who find theological concepts unproblematic and have problems grasping ethical concepts. Such people may feel very certain that God exists and commands his people and yet maintain that the notion of an ethics detached from religious authority eludes them. They may be troubled by the claim that ethical status involves possession of non-natural properties or pushed toward scepticism about the feasibility of philosophical theorizing in ethics by the seemingly inconclusive and interminable debates among the proponents of rival points of view. In short, perhaps what is successful as a philosophical analysis is person-relative, or at least relative to a conceptual scheme shared in its general features by the members of a community. And if conceptual priority is in this fashion context-relative, then it may be that a divine command theory does serve to clarify ethical concepts for certain groups of theists.

Leaving aside this admittedly speculative possibility, we can learn from the second objection that we need not regard our divine command theories as putative philosophical analyses. In this way we easily evade the objection.

III.3 *The Objection from Epistemic Asymmetries.* Some people think that various epistemic asymmetries count against divine command theories. For instance, people can come to know, or at least to believe with reason, that certain things are morally forbidden without also knowing, or having a reasonable belief, that such things are contrary to God's commands. Thus, a secular moralist might argue that slavery is morally forbidden because it degrades and dehumanizes its victims and yet might remain agnostic about whether God exists or, if he does, whether he forbids slavery. Moreover, even theists who claim that there is some connection between God's wishes and what ought to be donc often infer that something is commanded by God after first becoming convinced that it is required, morally speaking. A theist can, like anyone else, form his moral opinions by consulting his moral intuitions, conversing with casuists or reasoning from the principles of a favoured but non-theological ethical theory.

It is not altogether obvious what should be inferred from these asymmetries. After all, there seem to be matching asymmetries which favour the theologica! side of the equation. Sometimes theists at least claim that they infer what is morally required of them after first determining what God wills. Some theists set about confronting moral problems by seeking pastoral advice, studying scriptures, and praying for divine guidance, and this procedure suggests that they believe they can learn what they ought to do by discerning what God wants them to do. And it seems that people could come to know, or to believe with reason, that God had commanded certain things without also knowing, or believing reasonably, that such things were morally required. Thus, a theist might be very certain that God forbids the eating of pork while remaining in doubt about whether this is a moral prohibition or one that could be supported by recognizably moral reasons. So it seems that people act, or could act, as if the epistemic asymmetries in question were of little moment since they come in matched pairs.

A philosopher with a sceptical attitude about theology but not about ethics might advance the bold claim that, while it is epistemically possible to have independent justification for one's moral opinions, it is not epistemically possible for anyone to have a similar justification for his views about the divine will. At best this thesis is controversial, and even if it were true it does not seem to be an objection to any of the divine command theories we have formulated. Taken together with a divine command theory, the thesis only implies that the sole epistemic access we have to God's will and what he has commanded is through moral inquiry of the usual sort. Though I am inclined to suppppose that many theists would reject this view, even a divine command theorist could accept it with equanimity. If I have only a ruler, then the only way I can find out whether a certain triangular object is approximately equiangular may be first to measure its sides to determine whether it is approximately equilateral. But this restriction on my epistemic access to geometrical facts does nothing to falsify or undermine the necessary truth that something is an equilateral triangle if and only if it is an equiangular triangle. For similar reasons, it seems unreasonable to suppose that epistemic asymmetries could count against the principles of any divine command theory.

III.4   *The Objection from the Is–Ought Fallacy.* Many philosophers are convinced that it has been established that one cannot validly deduce an ought-statement from an is-statement. Hume is often cited as the person who added this item to the store of philosophical knowledge. However, it is by no means a simple task to turn this slogan into a precise and defensible doctrine. There are problems about how to draw the line between is-statements and ought-statements; care must be taken to rule out trivial counter-examples of the sort generated by the inferential rule of Disjunction Introduction; and a stand must be made on whether statements about institutional facts can be used to formulate genuine counter-examples to the claim.[12] Still, nuances apart, I suppose that some clear examples of the sort of fallacious inference the slogan is intended to call to our attention are available. Surely there would be a logical impropriety in deducing from a premiss of the form

(P) God commands that p.

a conclusion of the form

(C) It is required that p.

The inference from (P) to (C) seems to be about as obvious a *non sequitur* as one could hope to find.

But a problem arises if we try to convert this insight into a criticism of divine command theories. A divine command theorist will protest, and correctly so, that he does not deduce something like (C) from something like (P) alone. Rather he invokes one of the principles of his theory as an additional premiss in the argument. He may, for example, argue for

[12] The import of the problem of institutional facts is strikingly illustrated by the argument in John R. Searle's 'How to Derive "Ought" from "Is"', *The Philosophical Review* 73 (1964), pp. 43–58 and the abundant literature inspired by that paper.

something like (C) from something like (P) together with (T1a), and, if he does so, the argument will be valid. It is not clear whether mixed theological–ethical statements like the principles of our divine command theories are to be regarded as ought-statements or not. But what is quite obvious is that arguments whose premises include such statements plus is-statements about what God commands provide valid deductions of ought-statements about what is required, permitted, or forbidden.

Of course such arguments may be unsound; they will be if divine command theories are false. But we are engaged in hunting for reasons to believe that such theories are false and cannot just assume their falsity in the present context. The existence of a logical gap between facts and values does not by itself furnish such a reason, for the arguments whose invalidity is secured by this gap are ones which a careful divine command theorist need never invoke.

III.5   *The Euthyphro Objections.* What many modern philosophers take to be the earliest argument against divine command theories in Western philosophy is found in Plato's *Euthyphro.* Socrates asks whether the gods love holiness because it is holy or whether it is holy because the gods love it, and he persuades Euthyphro that holiness is loved by the gods because it is holy and that holiness is not holy because it is loved by the gods.[13] The argument used by Socrates to accomplish this is notoriously difficult to interpret. At times it seems that Socrates is only arguing that being holy and being loved by the gods are distinct properties. This seems to be a sane enough conclusion, but it would not perturb anyone who held one of our divine command theories. After all, the fact that equiangularity and equilaterality are distinct properties does not upset geometers who claim that the two are necessarily instantiated together. Moreover, as some translations have it, Socrates appears to be saying that the property of holiness itself has the property of being holy or that holiness instantiates itself. Like the claim that triangularity is triangular, this scarcely seems intelligible. If we were to try to reconstruct the authentic Socratic argument, we

---

[13] The question is posed in *Euthyphro* 10a, and the answer Socrates gives is stated in *Euthyphro* 10d.

might well run into insuperable difficulties in finding anything faintly plausible.[14]

However, the spirit of the Socratic contention seems to be embodied in a claim which can be translated into the terminology of our discussion with ease. It is this: Things are commanded by God because they are required and they are not required because they are commanded by God. This thesis is, as formulated, ambiguous by virtue of the different interpretations which the term 'because' will bear. At least two interpretations are worth discussing in some detail. One is causal, and the other has to do with reasons.

In discussing the causal interpretation, I shall take it for granted that we understand well enough for present purposes what it is for the obtaining of one state of affairs to cause or bring about the obtaining of another. On that interpretation, the two parts of the claim seem to amount to this:

(K1) A thing's being required brings about its being commanded by God.

(K2) It is not the case that a thing's being commanded by God brings about its being required.

And, of course, similar theses are to be understood as being asserted about the relations of the permitted and the forbidden to divine commands. A theist might well reject (K1) and its ilk on the grounds that, since God is free to command as he chooses, nothing other than God himself causes or brings about a thing's being commanded by God. But debate about whether or not one ought to accept theses like (K1) is peripheral to our concerns, for it is from (K2) and similar claims that a criticism of divine command theories can be launched. The argument can be fleshed out in the following way: (a) Suppose that a thing's being commanded by God does not bring about its being required; (b) Then it is causally possible that something is commanded by God and yet is not required; (c) Hence, it is logically possible that something is commanded by God but is not required; (d) Therefore, it is not necessary that if anything is commanded by God then it is required.

---

[14] An interesting recent attempt to extract an argument of some merit from this passage is Richard Sharvy's 'Euthyphro 9d–11b', Nous 6 (1972), pp. 119–37.

What the argument purports to show is that (K2) is inconsistent with (T1a). If this is so, a defender of T1 must reject (K2). Is this an unreasonable move to make? I cannot see that it is. It would seem that a defender of T1 might wish to assert that a thing's being commanded by God brings about its being required. After all, I can bring it about that I am required to do certain things by promising to do them. More to the point, an officer's command can bring it about that a private is required to do certain things. There is, it seems, nothing inherently confused about the general notion of bringing about requirements by command. To be sure, an officer's commands generate requirements only because an officer has the authority to command, and perhaps there are possible worlds in which God lacks whatever suffices to give a being moral authority. If so, the objection would constitute a difficulty for T1 but not necessarily for theories in the families of T2 and T3. It might well be that having made the universe (or being very powerful or loving human beings) is precisely what gives God moral authority. In any case, it would seem that a divine command theorist might well wish to hold that a thing's being commanded by a creator God (or by a loving or powerful God) does bring about its being required.

There is, moreover, another way in which the objection can be defeated, one which does not compel the divine command theorist to assert that divine commands cause requirements or to reject (K2). It is evident that one state of affairs can be a logically sufficient condition for another without the first also being a causally sufficient condition for the second. Thus, a person's being a bachelor is logically sufficient for that person's being unmarried, for it is necessary that if anything is a bachelor it is unmarried. But a person's being a bachelor does not bring about or cause that person's being unmarried. This, however, does not imply that it is causally possible for a bachelor to be married, for it is not even logically possible for a bachelor to be married. With this point in mind it is easy to formulate a reply to the objection. Let it be supposed that a thing's being commanded by God does not bring about its being required, as the first premiss of the objection has it. From this supposition it does not follow that it is causally or logically possible for something to be commanded by God and yet not required, as the second and third steps of the argument would have it. Hence, the reply to the objection consists in admitting the truth of its initial premiss but denying the validity of the objector's first inference from that premiss and also denying the truth of each subsequent assertion in the objector's argument. This is perhaps the most economical line of defence for a divine command theorist to adopt. He may simply note that none of the divine command theories we have formulated makes any causal claims, and so their proponents are as much entitled to assert negative causal principles like (K2) as is the imagined objector.

What the divine command theorist must insist upon is only that a thing's being commanded by God is at least a necessary part of a condition logically sufficient to insure its being required. Perhaps this claim is most plausible if restricted to circumstances in which God is creator, loving father, or powerful lord, but it is a consistent claim and one in the spirit of divine command theories even if not so restricted. In brief, in order to defeat this form of the objection our theorist can deny principles like (K2), that is, he can affirm that divine commands bring about requirements. It seems reasonable to suppose that some divine command theorists would do this. Alternatively, he can accept principles like (K2) and deny the validity of the inference his critic draws from them. Either way, the objection fails.

On the alternative interpretation, which has to do with reasons, the claim we are discussing has the following components:

(R1) A thing's being required is the reason for its being commanded by God.

(R2) It is not the case that a thing's being commanded by God is the reason for its being required.

A theist need not, I think, find the claim advanced by (R1) especially impressive, and could regard it with scepticism. He might acknowledge himself unable to fathom God's reasons for commanding what he does or even wonder whether there are reasons for divine commands. But some theists would surely find (R2) an attractive thesis, and it is (R2) which constitutes a threat to divine command theories. The precise nature of the threat is spelt out a bit in the following argument: (a) Suppose a thing's being commanded by God is not the reason for its being required; (b) Then there must be some reason other than God's commands why that thing is required; (c) But that reason might obtain even if God were not to command the thing in question; (d) Hence, it is possible that something is required but not commanded by God; (e) Therefore, it is not necessary that if a thing is required then it is commanded by God.

This argument, if successful, would be a powerful objection to divine command theories because its conclusion is the negation of (C_1), which is a constraint all our divine command theories were constructed to satisfy. Of course, a divine command theorist can consistently evade the objection by denying its first premiss and maintaining instead that the reason a thing is required is that it is commanded by God. Surely it would not be surprising to find a divine command theorist advancing such a claim. It has not, after all, been demonstrated that such a claim would be untenable, for the objector assumes but does not prove (R_2). But our theorist has another way around the difficulty, one which may seem more plausible once understood because it does not involve outright rejection of (R_2). There is a distinction to be drawn between a complete reason for something and part of a reason for that thing. A thing's having been commanded by God, it may be maintained, is not a complete reason for its being required, and so the initial supposition expressed by (R_2) is, in a sense, correct. Nevertheless, having been commanded by God is a part of some complete reason why things are required. What the remainder of a complete reason might be is open to dispute. Perhaps God's being our wise creator is the remainder, for we would surely owe obedience to the commands of a wise creator. Locke, at least, thought so at one time. He says:

And this obligation seems to derive partly from the divine wisdom of the law-maker, and partly from the right which the Creator has over His creation. For, ultimately, all obligation leads back to God and we are bound to show ourselves obedient to the authority of His will because both our being and our work depend on His will, since we have received these from Him, and so we are bound to observe the limits He prescribes; moreover, it is reasonable that we should do what shall please Him who is omniscient and most wise.[15]

Or perhaps God's being a loving father to us is the remainder, for it seems that we ought to do what a loving parent commands. But then our divine command theorist can claim that there is no complete reason for anything being required which does not include as a part that thing's having been commanded by God. In effect, he will deny the validity of the inference from the premiss

It is not the case that the complete reason for a thing's being required is its having been commanded by God.

to the conclusion

The complete reason for a thing's being required does not include as a part its having been commanded by God.

This inference, or something very much like it, seems needed to make the objection work, but its validity is at best doubtful.[16] If this is so, what is necessary is that if a thing is required then it is commanded by God, who has whatever other properties together with his commands provide complete reasons for requirements. Since exactly parallel arguments can be given in the cases of permissions and prohibitions, it is clear that this line of defence can be fitted comfortably within the framework of theories belonging to the families of T2 and T3. And so perhaps theories of these sorts have differentially greater plausibility than the simple theory T1. What should be emphasized, however, is that even T1 can be defended against the objection. A defender need only take care to insist that a thing's having been commanded by God is the complete reason why it is required. The objector has denied this, but he has assumed that it is not so rather than proving it. Since the objector's assumption is not obviously true, self-evident, or the

[15] Locke, op. cit., pp. 182–3.
[16] Baruch A. Brody has analysed a number of arguments which purport to show, in effect, that there must be complete reasons why things supposed to be commanded by God are required which do not include or make reference to their having been commanded by God. He builds a strong case for the conclusion that all the arguments he considers are unsound. See Baruch A. Brody, 'Morality and Religion Reconsidered', *Readings in the Philosophy of Religion* (ed. Baruch A. Brody), Englewood Cliffs: Prentice Hall (1974), pp. 592–603.

like, it does not seem that a divine command theorist would
fly in the face of reason by denying that assumption.

Thus, it seems safe to conclude that divine command theorists
can evade the objections from reasons and from causes. Perhaps
defenders of theories like T2 or T3 are on firmer ground in
doing so, but even a proponent of T1 can consistently get away
with such evasive tactics. A point worth special notice in light
of the fact that some philosophers are deeply committed to
principles like (K2) and (R2) is that some divine command
theories can escape the objections without recourse to denying
(K2) or one plausible version of (R2).

III.6 *The Objection from Prescriptive Force.* The view that
the words in our moral vocabulary are used to prescribe is
solidly established among modern ethical theorists.[17] To say
that it is required that Jones keeps his promises is, for example,
to prescribe a course of conduct for Jones. In the same manner,
claims that certain courses of action open to an agent are permitted or are forbidden are intended to guide or direct conduct. By contrast, an assertion that God commands something
or that he does not do so appears merely to state, if true, a
rather unusual fact. Thus, there is a deep and systematic
difference between the uses of our prescriptive and descriptive
vocabularies. Since this difference has to do with usage, or with
how the two vocabularies function in communication, it would
be appropriate to regard it as a difference in the logical features,
broadly speaking, of the two realms of language. In the light of
these logical differences, so the objection goes, it would be a
mistake to assert, as divine command theories do, logical
equivalences between propositions about divine commands
and propositions about moral requirements, permissions and
prohibitions.

There is much a divine command theorist could say about this
issue. Two points seem particularly worth a bit of discussion.
First, a divine command theorist can maintain that, within the
context of religious ethical discourse, statements about divine

---

[17] See R. M. Hare, *The Language of Morals*, Oxford: The Clarendon Press (1961).
Hare uses this feature of moral discourse as a basis for an interesting but controversial meta-ethical theory. I remain sceptical about some of Hare's theoretical
claims while acknowledging the sharpness of his insight into the way moral language
functions.

commands normally function to guide or direct action. It is not the case that statements of fact, couched in what is ostensibly a purely descriptive vocabulary, never have the function of guiding action. In some cases, the claim 'Your friends will disapprove!', which appears to be nothing more than a factual prediction, is intended and understood as an obliquely expressed directive. More significantly, theists normally take God to possess certain moral excellences; he is said to be supremely and perfectly good as well as just and merciful. With such theological doctrines as presuppositions or background assumptions, the theist has a reason for using statements about divine commands with prescriptive force, and so this logical feature is shared by both sides of the logical equivalences proposed by divine command theory. But, second, even if statements about God's commands were not by themselves used with prescriptive force, this would not establish the falsity of any of the theoretical principles of a divine command theory. Each such principle as a whole has prescriptive force in normal usage by virtue of the ethical terms contained in it, but this does not imply that each sentential part of every such principle must have this feature. After all, when something is prescribed, what is prescribed has to be described. If a hedonist asserts that something is good if and only if it produces a balance of pleasure over pain, he is commending something, and it is pleasure that he commends. Similarly, a divine command theorist is prescribing something, and it is obedience to God that he prescribes.

Hedonism may be an erroneous theory of value, and divine command theories may be mistaken about what is required of us. But neither is incorrect merely because its principles describe the kind of thing which is being commended or prescribed. We should, therefore, think of the principles of divine command theories as spelling out in some detail the general prescription of obedience to God's will and as apt for use in prescribing such obedience.

III.7 *The Objection from Universalizability*. It seems that moral judgements must be universalizable in some sense. Just what this amounts to is debatable and has turned out to be an interesting source of philosophical controversy. Roughly speaking, the thesis is that any moral judgement one makes in a particular situation of moral choice must also be made about any other situation which is similar in all morally relevant respects. Otherwise put, one must not make different moral judgements about actions which are exactly similar in every morally relevant respect. Presumably the point of requiring universalizability of moral judgements is to undercut the moral ground from arguments for exceptions to general moral rules in one's own favour or in favour of any particular person or group. Refusal to universalize is itself a moral fault. It is logically possible to make an exception in one's own case and people do it all too frequently, but no one should think or act in this fashion. According to the objection now to be considered, divine command theories confront a dilemma. Either the judgements derived from them are universalizable, or they are not. If they are, then general rules which prescribe innumerable obviously wicked actions are consequences of the theory; if they are not, exceptions to ordinary moral rules are allowed and this too is morally intolerable. In either case, the theories end up by promoting wickedness. Perhaps an example will clarify the point of the criticism. It certainly could have been the case that God commanded Abraham to kill Isaac, his innocent son, and if Scripture is to be believed, this is just what happened. Either Abraham's judgement that he is required to kill Isaac is universalizable or it is not. If it is, the consequence seems to be that anyone who can, ought to kill Isaac, or perhaps that everyone who cares to do so may kill their children, and these are surely repugnant conclusions. But, if it is not, then Abraham seems to be an exception to the general rule against slaughtering the innocent, which is an equally undesirable result. In either case, divine command theories seem to wind up by condoning or even encouraging evil.

Once the objection is stated this clearly, it becomes obvious how a divine command theorist ought to reply. He must admit that the judgements derived from his theory are universalizable but deny that this forces him to condone anything obviously immoral. Universalization, it will be recalled, is generalization over situations the same in all morally relevant respects. Concrete situations, of course, agree and disagree in innumerable respects, but not all of them are morally relevant. Divine command theories offer a particularly simple account of what is

morally relevant in comparing situations; as such theories
have it, the only morally relevant factor involved in similarity
judgements about actions is whether they have been commanded
by God, or by a powerful, loving or cosmogonic God. Other
respects in which actions may agree and differ, be they ever so
numerous and impressive, count not at all, morally speaking,
for such theories. This determines how Abraham's judgement
is correctly to be generalized. Thus, a divine command theorist
would have to allow that anyone who had been commanded by
God (or by a powerful, loving or creator God) to kill Isaac is
required to kill Isaac but not that anyone who can ought to kill
Isaac. And he would be quick to note that Scripture nowhere
suggests that anyone other than Abraham was so commanded.
Similarly, a divine command theorist would be constrained to
admit that everyone commanded by God (or by a powerful,
loving or creator God) to kill their children is required to do so
but not that everyone, whether appropriately commanded or
not, ought to act in this fashion. Surely divine command
theorists of sound mind would insist that few people, if any at
all, have actually been given such harsh commands. If we
decline to take Scripture literally on this point, perhaps no one
has ever been commanded by God to kill his son, and even if
Abraham is exceptional in being so commanded, he is not an
exception to a general rule. Since the general rule in question
is qualified by reference to divine commands, there is no reason
for a divine command theorist to believe, or for others to fear,
that widespread slaughter of the innocent will be prescribed
or in any way encouraged. Thus, some of the generalizations
gotten from divine command theories by universalizing particular moral judgements warranted by the theory may be very
limited in scope; maybe only one person is ever commanded by
God to perform a certain action. Depending on what, if
anything, God actually commands, these generalisations *may*
turn out not to differ at all from conventional moral wisdom.
If there are differences in rare cases like that of Abraham,
what is prescribed in those cases is not obviously immoral.
After all, it is not obvious, at least to many people who have
thought seriously about Abraham's situation, just what he
ought to have done. Both disobeying God and killing Isaac
seem to be intolerable, and all that seems really obvious

about the case is that Abraham was fortunate in avoiding both these outcomes.

Be that as it may, what emerges from the discussion is that divine command theories confront no logical problems in universalizing particular moral judgements; nor do they face moral problems of insurmountable difficulty. This is not exactly a surprising conclusion when one remembers that the theories themselves, as they have been formulated, are very general, and so it is only to be expected that universalization, if done correctly, will be consistent with these principles. In thinking about how to universalize within the context of a divine command theory one must take care to restrict generality to cases similar in respect to what God has commanded. Once this is done, the temptation to believe that divine command theories must prescribe innumerable wrong actions, or even a single obviously wicked action, vanishes.

III.8 *The Objection from Trivial Natural Theology.* According to yet another objection, if we were to accept a divine command theory, the main task of natural theology, proving the existence of God, would become trivially easy to accomplish instead of being, as it should, difficult if not impossible. In order to see why this might be so, consider the following argument:

(1) For some q, it is required that q.
(2) Necessarily, for all p, it is required that p iff God commands that p.
(3) Hence, for some q, God commands that q.
(4) Therefore, God exists.

Certainly it must be conceded that this argument is formally valid. Moreover, almost everyone would admit the truth of the claim that there are some moral requirements, which is what the first premiss asserts. If we then also acknowledge the truth of the principle of T1 governing requirements, which is expressed by the second premiss, we are thereby committed to allowing that the argument is sound and its conclusion is true. A parallel argument can, of course, be constructed using the principle of T1 which governs prohibitions, and similar but slightly more complex arguments of the same sort can be constructed from those principles of T2 and T3 which deal with requirements and prohibitions. In short, an argument like the one we are considering will be sound if a divine command theory is true provided only that some things are either required or forbidden. So it seems that a divine command theorist has a simple way to prove the existence of God, a way so simple that it will produce only suspicion and never conviction. Given the evident validity of the argument, any doubts about its conclusion would direct suspicion towards its second premiss for most people, though an odd character here and there might be persuaded by such doubts to question its first premiss. In any case, it does not seem reasonable to allow that arguments like this one could be said to prove the existence of God. But, if a divine command theory is true, they seem to prove just that. Therefore, it seems unreasonable to admit that a divine command theory could be true.

To counter this objection a divine command theorist can invoke the general doctrine that not every sound argument is in any useful sense a proof of its conclusion.[18] Consider, for instance, the following argument:

(5) There are human persons.
(6) Either there are no human persons or God exists.
(7) Hence, God exists.

As was the previous argument, this one is obviously valid, and its first premiss would be admitted by almost everybody. If we then acknowledge the truth of its second premiss, we are thereby committed to admitting its soundness and the truth of its conclusion. But even a convinced theist, who will believe this argument to be sound, need not admit that it proves the existence of God, and it is extremely doubtful that very many theists would regard it as a successful proof of the existence of God. Why it is not successful turns out to be a rather difficult question to answer. Perhaps we could say, by way of a vague but intuitively plausible answer, that this is because the proposition expressed by (6) does not have epistemic priority over the proposition expressed by (7) or, what comes to much the same thing, because what (6) asserts is not, apart from the argument

---

[18] There is discussion of valid arguments, which may also be sound, but which by no stretch of the imagination prove the existence of God, in George I. Mavrodes, *Belief in God*, New York: Random House (1970).

in question, better justified than what (7) asserts for ordinary epistemic subjects or even for theists. Precisely the same gambit can be used by the divine command theorist in his response to the previous argument. Someone who is both a theist and a divine command theorist will believe that argument to be sound, but such a person is not forced to claim also that it proves the existence of God. The reason the argument is not a proof, it may be maintained, is that what (2) asserts is not, apart from the argument in question, better justified for the ordinary epistemic subject, or, for that matter, for the divine command theorist himself, than what (4) asserts. This does not mean it would be unreasonable to believe what (2) asserts, as the objection has it, only that it would not be more reasonable to believe what (2) asserts than to believe what (4) asserts. And this is why, the divine command theorist may claim, the original argument, though it may be sound as he believes, is not a proof of the existence of God. Therefore, the validity or even the soundness of arguments like our first argument would not trivialize natural theology in the way the objector thinks it would.

III.9   *The Objection from Intuition.* As a last resort, someone who wishes to reject divine command theories may fall back on his intuitions. It is, of course, notorious that moral intuitions fail to produce agreement about controversial issues, as recent actual cases involving abortion, euthanasia and similar problems show quite clearly. So a divine command theorist might be understandably unimpressed by an appeal to intuition on the part of his critics.

In addition, if the critic is to deploy intuitions against these theories, he will probably have to go beyond actual moral problems into the realm of the merely possible. The reason for this is easy to see. Suppose the critic invokes the intuition that gratuitous cruelty is morally forbidden. This will not upset the divine command theorist; he will agree, adding that such cruelty is contrary to the commands of God, who is our creator and loving father. So the critic must take the next step and maintain that gratuitous cruelty would also be forbidden in various hypothetical and counterfactual circumstances. If arguing against T1, the critic is obliged to assert a counterfactual like the following:

If God had commanded what we call 'gratuitous cruelty' (and not also its negation), then what we call 'gratuitous cruelty' would still have been morally forbidden and not morally required.

against the defender of T1, who will assert:

If God had commanded what we call 'gratuitous cruelty' (and not also its negation), then what we call 'gratuitous cruelty' would have been morally required and not morally forbidden.

So it is clear that intuitions which agree about actual cases may diverge when brought to bear on counterfactual cases. What is not so obvious is whether this conflict of intuitions can be resolved by intuitions and, if so, how this is to be done. According to a recent theory about counterfactuals, when we wish to determine whether or not counterfactual conditionals are true, we are supposed to think about possible worlds of greatest over-all similarity to the actual world in which their antecedents are true and then try to figure out whether their consequents are true in those worlds.[19] No doubt there are cases in which following these instructions will yield results which have widespread intuitive plausibility. If we are trying to decide whether

If Professor Freud had promised to grade Betty's paper today, he would be obliged to do so.

or whether instead

If Professor Freud had promised to grade Betty's paper today, he would still not be obliged to do so.

we may imagine that intuition decides the case in favour of the former claim. After all, possible worlds in which the Professor makes the promise he did not make in the actual world may differ very little from the actual world, and the points of difference may have nothing much to do with how people acquire obligations. But it is not to be expected that such a fortunate outcome should occur in every case. Possible worlds with the

---

[19] See David Lewis, *Counterfactuals*, Oxford: Basil Blackwell (1973), especially Section 4.2 on the vagueness of the notion of over-all similarity. Actually, the theory Lewis proposes is primarily a theory about the truth-conditions for counterfactuals and not a theory about how we can discover which counterfactuals are true. Speaking as I do as if it were a theory about the epistemology of counterfactuals is intended only to be heuristically suggestive.

greatest over-all similarity to the actual world in which God commands what we call 'gratuitous cruelty' might yet be very unlike the actual world, so dissimilar that intuition is an unreliable guide to what is required and what forbidden there. It might be, for example, that in such worlds what we call 'gratuituous cruelty' provides cathartic release for its perpetrators without causing pain to its victims, for over-all similarity is not necessarily tied to sameness of causal laws. And the respects in which such worlds differ from the actual world might have a great deal to do with how things acquire moral status. Perhaps, then, it would be excessive to assume that the critic's intuitions about the morality in such worlds will be invariably correct. At the very least, there seems to be no reason why a divine command theorist should subscribe to a view which licenses moral dogmatism on the part of his critics. Indeed, since the divine command theorist holds that the difference between God's commands between the actual world and such possible worlds is just what makes a difference in the moral order between worlds, he will have some reason to think that his critic's intuitions about the moral order in such possible worlds are faulty. If the critic insists that his intuitions about the matter must settle the question, then surely our divine command theorist can with justification reply that this tactic begs the question against intuitions shaped by and congruent with divine command theories. At the very least, it seems incumbent on the critic to provide a theoretical rationale for his judgement about the moralities in possible worlds, something which goes beyond the bare appeal to intuition. Perhaps the critic has not seriously entertained the counterfactual's antecedent because he cannot bring himself to suppose, even hypothetically, that God exists and issues commands.

When we consider theories like T2 and T3 things are much the same, except that the thought-experiments are more complicated because we must think about possible worlds in which a creator God issues bizarre commands and yet over-all similarities with the actual world are maximized. As before, the divine command theorist's line of defence is a sceptical attitude toward the epistemic authority of his critic's moral intuitions about such worlds, if indeed the critic professes to have any intuitions at all about such hypothetical circumstances. In general, the divine command theorist can distrust moral intuitions which are not anchored in actuality or tied very closely to it and can allow his theory to decide matters with reference to remote possibilities in so far as anything at all needs to be said about them. Thus he is able, consistently and with some reason, to turn aside the objection.

III.10 *Practical Objections.* A moral theory is occasionally criticized by trying to show that, even if it were true, bad consequences would ensue if it were generally believed. Unless one believes that discovering truth is more valuable than any other human activity and possessing truth is worth whatever it may cost, a successful criticism of this sort would provide some reason for thinking that believing the theory in question should not be encouraged, though it would furnish no reason for assuming that the theory is false or indefensible. Some objections of this variety can be raised against divine command theories. If one of them is cogent, perhaps one should refrain from defending such theories even if they can be successfully defended. Two particular objections are worth some attention.

According to the first, widespread belief in divine command theories is likely to contribute to moral libertinism in present cultural circumstances. It is not too hard to understand why this might be the case. Since divine command theories do not entail that God exists, it is possible for a person both to be an atheist and to hold a divine command theory. Someone who took such a position would, depending on which divine command theory he held, believe either that everything is permitted or that nothing is required, forbidden, or permitted. Many of us have known people who, after losing religious faith and ceasing to believe in God, pass through a period of libertinism. It is tempting to suppose that this can be accounted for by saying that such folk act as if they had ceased to be theists but still thought about morals from the point of view of a divine command theory. Fortunately, such crises are often only temporary and terminate when the patient has reconstructed a personal moral code based on non-theological assumptions. Since it seems to be the case that traditional theism is on the wane at least among certain influential groups in industrial societies, it is to some degree probable that large numbers of people will come to act in these deplorable ways, either temporarily or permanently. Should this happen, such people would constitute a threat to good morals in a community and a menace to social order. Indeed, it is arguable that such a process has been going on for well over a century and has been acutely portrayed and correctly diagnosed in the novels of Dostoevksy. And, if the gradual retreat of theism is a more or less inevitable historical trend, as some people believe, then it would seem to be sound social policy to discourage belief in divine command theories even among theists, lest those among them who do lose their faith run amok in the period before they reach a new point of moral equilibrium.

The second objection advances the claim that general belief in divine command theories, or in any theory according to which moral principles are logically dependent upon theological assumptions, is likely to encourage both unnecessary moral controversy and ethical scepticism. The argument for this claim is fairly direct. It may be doubted whether there has ever been an agreed-upon method for establishing any one set of religious beliefs against the proponents of other religions or of irreligion; in particular, controversy over what God has commanded may be both futile and interminable. If this is so, then there is nothing to be gained by insisting that morality must be grounded in, or dependent on, religion. All the difficulties involved in dealing with religious controversies in a rational fashion would be injected into moral debate, and once this had happened the prospects for reaching consensus about some moral principles would probably be diminished and ethical scepticism might well be encouraged among those who could not conscientiously adhere to religious beliefs of the appropriate kind. Therefore, if religious ethics is a source of moral discord, then it would seem to be prudent not to foster belief in divine command theories and their kin and to hope that moral agreement and social harmony can be founded on a firmer and less controversial basis.[20]

Needless to say, a convinced defender of a divine command

---

[20] Considerations of this sort are discussed in William K. Frankena's 'Is Morality Logically Dependent on Religion?', *Religion and Morality* (ed. Gene Outka and John P. Reeder, Jr.), Garden City: Doubleday (1973), pp. 295–317. Frankena holds that if the view that morality depends on reglion rested on good grounds we should have to espouse it. Would we? He also thinks this view does not rest on good grounds.

theory will find neither objection persuasive. He may judge the threat portrayed in the first objection to have been too melodramatically treated to seem realistic. No doubt loss of faith can produce a psychological crisis which infests the moral life, but it would be a breath-taking simplification to imagine that such moral excesses as do occur in these episodes are to be attributed to anything so esoteric as the holding of a divine command theory. As for policy, the divine command theorist, who is typically a theist himself, can insist that the interests of truth, good morals, and social order can best be served by encouraging general belief in theism and some version of divine command theory. From his point of view, discouraging belief in divine command theories must seem, at best, the unhappy expedient to which societies that have lost the ability or the will to inculcate proper religion in their members may find it prudent to resort. Nor need the divine command theorist be greatly dismayed by the prospect of moral controversy suggested by the second objection. Within the context of divine command theories like those we have discussed, moral issues will be neither more nor less controversial than religious issues for reasons of symmetry. Of course, from disagreements about God's commands there can be derived disagreements about requirements, permissions and prohibitions, but agreements about the former issues will also lead to agreements about the latter. And, symmetrically, agreements about what God commands can be derived from agreements about the moral issues thereby allowing moral consensus to have leverage in resolving religious controversy, though disagreements about the moral issues will lead to disagreements about what God commands thereby exacerbating religious controversy. It is, to be sure, open to question whether or not discussion should be conducted within the context of any divine command theory, and there will always be those who are incredulous with respect to such theories. However, in this regard divine command theories differ not at all from other ethical theories such as utilitarian theories, which are also questionable and viewed with frank disbelief by some people. Some philosophers are inclined to suppose that divine command theories must be more controversial than other ethical theories because the objections to them are weightier than the objections to other theories, but our examination of these objections provides no support for this philosophical prejudice.

4

There are, then, several distinct divine command theories. The various theories, and perhaps others we have not considered, are different in the perfectly ordinary sense of having different consequence classes, that is, different sets of theorems. The moral to be drawn from this is that, in discussing divine command theories, we should take care to specify which one is being attacked or defended.

If my treatment of the critical dialectic has been fair and accurate, each of these theories can be consistently defended against the standard arguments philosophers have put forth in criticism of divine command theories. As one would expect, the plausibility of the defence varies with the theory being defended. Though theories in the families of T2 and T3 may fare better than T1, particularly in their ability to cope with the *Euthyphro* Objection, even T1 is not conclusively refuted by any of the objections we have considered. The upshot is that it has not been shown beyond reasonable doubt that divine command theories are false. This is, I think, a modest enough conclusion, but even so some people are sure to find it outrageous.

Perhaps the sense of outrage will be somewhat abated by the observation that nothing I have said tends to show that any divine command theory is plausible or worthy of acceptance. In replying to objections, I have not endeavoured to establish even the slightest presumption in favour of a divine command theory. For all I know, divine command theories are only plausible relative to certain theological doctrines which themselves are philosophically unjustified and maybe even unjustifiable. Like the fabled plain man confronted with certain sceptical theories of the philosophers, the ordinary philosopher confronted with the divine command theories of the theologians may find that they produce astonishment but no conviction. It may be that certain believers have evidence which supports one or another divine command theory, or at least think they do. Such people might be comforted by the thought that holding a divine command theory is not a philosophically indefensible position, for there does not seem to be any obvious, self-evident, or indisputable doctrine contained in our philosophical lore which would serve to make divine command theories untenable. Those of us who lack such evidence about religion but who also fall short of having enough evidence to place some alternative theory, inconsistent with all divine command theories, beyond reasonable doubt, should, I think, adopt the cautious policy of suspending judgement on divine command theories, neither accepting them nor rejecting them, at least in the context of theoretical discussion. And if there are philosophers who find the suspense intolerable, they should, if they can, invent some arguments which will refute divine command theories more convincingly than has heretofore been done.

For my part, I confess I once believed that, no matter what the fate of other theological doctrines, divine command theories must be false. I was awakened from my dogmatic slumber on this point when I began to study the arguments examined above. Perhaps divine command theories can be refuted, but at present I do not see just how this remarkable feat is to be accomplished. The inability conclusively to falsify divine command theories may, of course, be regarded as merely illustrating Quine's general doctrine that any theoretical statement can be held true come what may provided we are willing to make suitable adjustments elsewhere in the system of our beliefs.[21] What I find interesting, and a bit surprising, is that only minimal adjustments are needed to defend divine command theories against objections and that these adjustments have an air of plausibility, at least relative to a conceptual framework which we may presume is shared by many theists.

[21] W. V. O. Quine, 'Two Dogmas of Empiricism', *From a Logical Point of View*, New York: Harper & Row (1963), p. 43.

III

Some
Divine Command Theories

Up to this point my argument has been mainly a defence of certain propositions central to divine command theories of ethics. Those propositions are to be regarded as the kernels of such theories, but the theological kernel of a divine command theory is a rather meagre thing. It must somehow be embedded in a theoretical context which will have the logical power and richness to permit us to formulate definitions of many of the usual ethical concepts and to deduce from the fundamental principles of the theory consequences which exhibit the relations among those concepts. Only when this has been done will we have before us a body of doctrine worthy of being called 'a divine command theory'. Since, as I have taken pains to emphasize, there are alternative kernels which might be incorporated into such a theory, we will find that there are also several distinct divine command theories of ethics. In this chapter I propose to formulate some of them. In order to achieve clarity of exposition I shall proceed in axiomatic fashion. Starting from a few primitive notions, some definitions and a few axioms, we will construct step by step some rather elaborate theory which incorporates the divine command theorist's assumptions about the relations between God's commands and several kinds of moral status. As the construction progresses, we shall also discuss some of the philosophical problems which can be usefully examined in the light of our postulates. In order to reduce the notational complexity of our formulations we shall drop the necessity operators and universal quantifiers which, as in the previous chapter, prefixed the formulas that expressed our core theoretical assertions.

The theories I propose to consider may be thought of as consisting of two tiers or levels. The first level is concerned with matters of moral worth or value, and so it might be thought of as axiological in nature. The familiar concepts to be accounted for at this level of theory construction are the morally good, bad, and indifferent. One unfamiliar and extraordinary concept must be added to these to get a logically exhaustive set of categories; the novel category defined for these purposes will be called, appropriately enough, 'the extraordinary'.

We begin by assuming some formulation of the propositional calculus. To this we add the primitive locution 'It ought to be the case that p', symbolized 'Op'. In terms of this locution we may define the other basic terms of this tier of our theory as follows:

(D1) $Gp = Def\ Op\ \&\ \sim O \sim p$
(D2) $Bp = Def\ O \sim p\ \&\ \sim Op$
(D3) $Ip = Def \sim Op\ \&\ \sim O \sim p$
(D4) $Ep = Def\ Op\ \&\ O \sim p$.

The readings which are intended for the pieces of uninterpreted notation in the first three definitions are these: 'Gp' is to abbreviate 'It would be good that p', 'Bp' is to stand for 'It would be bad that p' and 'Ip' is to mean 'It would be indifferent that p.' There seems to be no expression of ordinary English that captures exactly the sense of 'Ep', perhaps because it is generally supposed that no proposition satisfies (D4), and so I shall stipulate that it is to be read as 'It would be extraordinary that p.' Let us also read 'Mp' as 'It is possible that p' and 'Np' as 'It is necessary that p,' and then we may assume the usual definition connecting these two modal concepts:

(D5) $Np = Def \sim M \sim p$.

We will find that (D5) will prove useful in establishing connections between what ought to be the case and what is possible. From (D1)–(D4) plus propositional calculus we may infer that our four defined ethical categories are collectively exhaustive:

(T1) $Gp\ v\ Bp\ v\ Ip\ v\ Ep$.

We may also infer that these categories are mutually exclusive:

(T2) $\sim Gp \equiv Bp \; v \; Ip \; v \; Ep$
(T3) $\sim Bp \equiv Ip \; v \; Ep \; v \; Gp$
(T4) $\sim Ip \equiv Ep \; v \; Gp \; v \; Bp$
(T5) $\sim Ep \equiv Gp \; v \; Bp \; v \; Ip.$

Hence, the good, the bad, the indifferent, and the extraordinary comprise a complete set of categories defined in terms of our primitive ethical notion.

Next we add to our definitions the following two axioms:

(A1) $Op \equiv O \sim \sim p$
(A2) $Op \supset Mp.$

Since any proposition is logically equivalent to its own double negation, it seems evident that (A1) expresses an axiomatic truth. With (A2) we express a pale reflection of the principle that 'ought' implies 'can'; the reflection is pale because what is logically possible may yet be past and unalterable and, hence, beyond the power of anyone to bring about or to prevent. All that (A2) asserts is that everything which ought to be is logically possible.

From our definitions plus (A1) and propositional calculus we can deduce the following theorems:

(T6) $Gp \equiv B \sim p$
(T7) $Bp \equiv G \sim p$
(T8) $Ip \equiv I \sim p$
(T9) $Ep \equiv E \sim p.$

The negation of something good is something bad, and the negation of something bad is something good. In this sense, the categories of the good and the bad may be conceived as 'mirror-images' or 'reflections' of one another. By contrast, the negation of something indifferent is also indifferent, and the negation of something extraordinary is itself extraordinary. Thus the categories of the indifferent and the extraordinary are such that each is its own reflection under negation. From (A2) plus propositional calculus we may also deduce:

(T10) $\sim Mp \supset \sim Gp$
(T11) $Np \supset \sim Bp.$

These theorems tell us that nothing impossible is good and that nothing necessary is bad. This is surely as things should be. Some people might suppose that both the necessary and the impossible are indifferent. Doubtless some necessary truths, for instance, that two plus two equals four, are morally indifferent. But some propositions, for instance, the proposition that God exists, are either necessary or impossible according to many people and yet are good and have bad negations. Hence, stronger conclusions than those expressed by (T10) and (T11) do not seem to be warranted.

Let us envisage now turning the theory elaborated so far into a doctrine with theological import. Let 'Wp' abbreviate 'God wishes that p.' Alternative readings are: 'God wants it to be the case that p', 'God would have it that p' or even 'God desires that p.' I intend this locution to be understood in such a way that God, if he exists, need not command all that he wishes for. Thus God may wish that we all be perfect in charity without commanding so much. The appropriate axiom linking God's wishes and what ought to be would seem to be the following:

(A3) $Op \equiv Wp$.

With the aid of (A2) and (A3) together we may conclude that God's wishes are circumscribed by the laws of logic and do not run beyond what is logically possible:

(T12) $\sim Mp \supset \sim Wp$
(T13) $Np \supset \sim W \sim p$
(T14) $\sim W(p \And \sim p)$.

God wishes only for what is possible. He does not hanker after contradictory things or other impossibilities, nor does he wish for the negation of what is necessary. These are encouragingly plausible conclusions. Moreover, we may also derive these consequences from (A3):

(T15) $Gp \equiv Wp \And \sim W \sim p$
(T16) $Bp \equiv W \sim p \And \sim Wp$
(T17) $Ip \equiv \sim Wp \And \sim W \sim p$
(T18) $Ep \equiv Wp \And W \sim p$.

Anything good is such that God wishes for it and does not wish for its negation. Anything bad is such that God does not wish for it but does wish for its negation. Anything indifferent is such that God neither wishes for it nor wishes for its negation; God does not care one way or the other about the indifferent. Finally, anything extraordinary is such that God both wishes for it and wishes for its negation.

Let us now take a closer look at the relations among the three familiar categories: the good, the bad, and the indifferent. We can easily prove the following theorems:

(T19) $Gp \supset \sim(Bp \lor Ip)$
(T20) $Bp \supset \sim(Gp \lor Ip)$
(T21) $Ip \supset \sim(Gp \lor Bp)$.

According to (T19), if anything is good, it is neither bad nor indifferent, but something not good need not be bad or indifferent since such a thing might be extraordinary. According to (T20), if anything is bad, it is neither good nor indifferent, and (T21) tells us that if anything is indifferent it is neither good nor bad. But, for all we have said so far, what is not bad need not be either good or indifferent, and what is not indifferent need not be good or bad. In either case, the extraordinary remains a possiblity.

Shall we eliminate this possibility by postulation? It would be ruled out if we were to adopt the following axiom:

(A4)* $Op \supset \sim O\sim p$.

But (A4), though a common enough assumption, has recently come under fire from philosophical critics.[1] (I have marked (A4) and will mark those theorems whose proofs employ it with an asterisk to indicate their problematic status.) Consider the case of Antigone. Perhaps, when all is said and done, the tragedy of her situation is that it ought to be that she buries her brother, and it ought to be that she does not bury her brother. Her tragedy may lie, at least in part, in the fact that her case is extraordinary. And, as van Fraassen has noted, the cases of Orestes, Ibsen's Nora, and Sartre's young man who must choose between joining the Resistance and caring for his mother all suggest a similar lesson.[2] So we should hesitate before adopting (A4).

[1] Bas C. van Fraassen, 'Values and the Heart's Command', *The Journal of Philosophy* 70 (1973), pp. 5–19.
[2] Ibid., pp. 9–11.

If we were to postulate (A4), our theory would gain a good deal by way of simplicity. Some of the consequences of (A4) are worth making explicit. The first consequence of note is that the good, the bad, and the indifferent become collectively exhaustive:

(T22)* Gp v Bp v Ip.

Since this is the case, we may strengthen the results expressed by (T19)–(T21) in the following way:

(T23)* ~Gp ≡ (Ip v Bp)
(T24)* ~Bp ≡ (Gp v Ip)
(T25)* ~Ip ≡ (Gp v Bp).

In short, given (A4), the good, the bad, and the indifferent comprise a mutually exclusive and collectively exhaustive set of categories defined in terms of our primitive locution of moral value. Further consequences of (A4) are these:

(T26)* Gp ≡ Op
(T27)* Bp ≡ O~p.

And the main theological consequences of (A4) are the following:

(T28)* Gp ≡ Wp
(T29)* Bp ≡ W~p
(T30)* ~(Wp & W~p).

Something is good just in case God would have it be the case, and something is bad just in case God would have its negation be the case. Moreover, God does not wish for something and wish for its negation. This last conclusion is, perhaps, dubious theology because of the restriction it imposes on God's desires. If so, the fact that (T30) is a consequence of (A4) might be looked at as another reason for rejecting (A4). After all, it may be that God would have it that Abraham kills Isaac and God would have it that Abraham does not kill Isaac.

In summary, we may describe the axiological tier of our theory as leaving open two possibilities. If we refrain from postulating (A4), we can deduce from the remaining definitions and axioms (T1)–(T21). If we add (A4) to the rest, we can also deduce theorems (T22)–(T30). Our decision about (A4) will determine whether the category of the extraordinary is empty and, hence, whether there is a fourfold partition of the class of all propositions by our categories of value or whether the partition is only threefold.

However, it should be pointed out that the theory we have set forth may be regarded as incomplete in various ways. We have not, for example, laid down any axioms governing the interaction of our primitive locution with sentential connectives such as conjunction. What should we say, for instance, about the question of whether each of the conjuncts in a conjunction that ought to be also ought to be? It might be supposed that a plausible assumption is the following:

(Op & Oq) ⊃ O (p & q).

But this principle, together with (A2), allows us to deduce (A4) upon substitution of '∼p' for 'q'. Since there are grounds for doubting (A4), we ought to hesitate to postulate this principle. Or, we might imagine it is reasonable to assume:

O (p & q) ⊃ (Op & Oq).

Again there are reasons to doubt. Some have supposed that it is on balance good that there are slight sufferings which evoke the tender care of good samaritans. If this is the case, then by (D1) it ought to be that there is suffering and suffering evokes the pity of good samaritans. But even so it ought not to be the case that there is suffering, and we have, therefore, what would appear to be a counter-example to the proposed principle.

Nor, to give another example, have we proposed any axioms governing iterated applications of the sentential operator which expresses our primitive ethical notion. What should we say on this topic? It may be that we should suppose:

Op ⊃ OOp.

But perhaps not. Though it ought to be that suffering is relieved, if there ought not to be any suffering, then it may be that it ought not to be that it ought to be that suffering is relieved. Perhaps what we should assume is rather this:

OOp ⊃ Op.

But, again, maybe not. Suppose that it ought to be that it

ought to be that no one punishes wrongdoers because if things were as they ought to be there would be no wrongdoers. Still, since there are wrongdoers, it ought not to be that no one punishes wrongdoers. Once again we have what some people would be inclined to take to be a plausible counter-example to the proposed principle.

Because I am not sure just which principles governing conjunction and iteration, or, for that matter, regulating disjunction and material implication, should be added to our theory, I will leave the question open at this point. It then becomes a topic for further discussion and thought, or for the reader's preference, to decide which such principles are worthy of adoption, provided they are consistent with what has already been assumed. For our purposes, things are complicated enough as they are, and the only crucial point to be made here is that our theory can be strengthened by adding to its axioms.

2

On top of the axiological tier of our theory, as it were, we wish to erect a deontological layer. While axiology has to do with what is, morally speaking, good, bad or indifferent (and perhaps extraordinary as well), deontology has to do with what the moral law requires, forbids, and permits. As a primitive locution for the upper level of our theoretical edifice we will take the expression 'It is obligatory that p', symbolized as 'Lp'. Alternative readings of the symbolic expression are: 'The moral law imposes the obligation that p' or 'The moral law imposes the requirement that p'. In terms of this primitive notion we may lay down the following definitions:

(D6) $Rp = \text{Def } Lp$
(D7) $Fp = \text{Def } L\sim p$
(D8) $Pp = \text{Def}\sim L\sim p.$

In (D6) the expression 'Rp' is to be read as 'It is required that p'; in (D7), 'Fp' is to abbreviate 'It is forbidden that p'; and in (D8), 'Pp' is to stand for 'It is permitted that p'. From these definitions we may, using only propositional calculus, infer the following theorems:

(T31) $Pp \text{ v } Fp$
(T32) $Pp \equiv \sim Fp.$

The permitted and the forbidden are mutually exclusive and collectively exhaustive categories. We may then, without any hesitation, affirm the appropriate analogue of (A1) for our new primitive notion:

(A5) $Lp \equiv L\sim\sim p$.

With the aid of (A5) we are able to deduce two additional theorems of some importance:

(T33) $Rp \equiv F\sim p$
(T34) $Fp \equiv R\sim p$.

The required and the forbidden are 'mirror-images' or 'reflections' of one another under negation in the sense that a proposition falls into one of these categories just in case its negation falls into the other. What has so far been left unsettled is the relation between the required and the permitted. Is everything required also permitted, or are there things which are required but not permitted? We shall return to this question later on in the discussion.

It is evident that we need to adopt principles which establish connections between the two levels of our theory. One which is clearly unproblematic is this:

(A6) $Lp \supset Op$.

Surely if something is obligatory, then it ought to be the case. We should not, however, also assume that if something ought to be the case then it is obligatory, for to do so would amount to collapsing the distinction between our axiology and our deontology. We wish to allow that there may be things which ought to be, but are not, obligatory, for instance, supererogatory actions.

From (A6), together with our other assumptions, we can deduce some rather interesting theorems:

(T35) $Ip \supset (Pp \ \& \ P\sim p)$
(T36) $Ip \supset (\sim Rp \ \& \ \sim R\sim p)$
(T37) $Ip \supset (\sim Fp \ \& \ \sim F\sim p)$.

If a proposition is indifferent, both it and its negation are permitted and neither is either required or forbidden. Since, according to (T21), the indifferent is neither good nor bad, we may conclude that the indifferent constitutes what is, so to speak, outside the moral realm. Presumably most of us believe that some things, for example, the proposition that Copernicus yawns, are morally indifferent in this sense. Other relations between our axiological and our deontological concepts which can be inferred with the help of (A6) are these:

(T38) $Gp \supset Pp$
(T39) $Bp \supset \sim Rp.$

According to (T38), anything good is also permitted. When we couple this result with (T35), we discover that whatever is either good or indifferent is also permitted. But, for all we have said thus far, there may be bad things, or even extraordinary things, which are permitted as well. According to (T39), nothing bad is required. Coupling this result with (T36), we learn that whatever is either bad or indifferent is not required. But there may also be, for all we have yet said, good things, or even extraordinary things, which are not required either. Among the consequences of (A2) and (A6), taken together, are these:

(T40) $Rp \supset Mp$
(T41) $Np \supset \sim Fp.$

What is required is possible, and so, by contraposition, what is impossible is not required. Moreover, what is necessary is not forbidden and, hence, is permitted. These seem to be sensible principles, ones most of us would wish to have governing the relations between the deontic and alethic modalities. Finally, (A6) allows us to deduce these two theorems:

(T42) $Rp \supset (Gp \lor Ep)$
(T43) $Fp \supset (Bp \lor Ep).$

What is required is also either good or extraordinary, and what is forbidden is either bad or extraordinary.

As noted above, (A6) leaves open the possibility that there are things which are good but not required. Letting 'Sp' abbreviate 'It is supererogatory that p' and 'Dp' stand for 'It is discreditable that p', we may accommodate the possibility in terms of this pair of definitions:

(D9) $Sp = Def\ Gp\ \&\ \sim Rp$

(D10) Dp = Def Bp & Pp.

The supererogatory is what is good but not required, and the discreditable is what is bad but permitted. The supererogatory and the discreditable are reflections of one another under negation in the sense that the negation of a proposition which falls into one of these categories falls into the other, as the next two theorems assure us:

(T44) Sp ≡ D~p
(T45) Dp ≡ S~p.

Thus, it might be supererogatory that Jones looks after the lunatics in Bedlam. If so, it would be good but not required that Jones does this work of mercy. In that case, it would be bad but permitted that Jones does not perform this act of moral heroism, and, hence, it would be discreditable that Jones does not look after the lunatics in Bedlam. Similarly, if it is discreditable that I continue to smoke cigarettes, then it is supererogatory that I do not continue to smoke them.

We can inject theological doctrine into the deontological doctrine formulated so far by equating what is commanded by God with what the moral law makes obligatory. Let 'Cp' abbreviate 'God commands that p'. The appropriate axiom will then be the following:

(A7) Cp ≡ Lp.

What (A7) tells us is that something is obligatory just in case God commands it. From (A7) and (D6)–(D8) we may infer the following important theorems:

(T46) Rp ≡ Cp
(T47) Fp ≡ C~p.
(T48) Pp ≡ ~C~p.

These theorems guarantee that the theory we are presently engaged in constructing is a divine command theory in the sense fixed upon earlier. Since (T46)–(T48) are the same as (T1a)–(T1c) in the second chapter minus the outer necessity operators and quantifiers, these theorems in our present theory are logical consequences of the kernel of a simple divine command theory as set forth in that chapter. Hence, we may say that our present theory is a non-modal version of a simple divine command theory. And, of course, we could obtain the modal version of the theory by prefixing all our axioms with universal quantifiers and necessity operators at the cost of a slight increase in notational complexity. But there are other, perhaps more interesting, consequences which can be drawn from our theory with the aid of (A7). Some of them are the following:

(T49) $Cp \supset Wp$
(T50) $Cp \supset Mp$
(T51) $Np \supset \sim C \sim p$
(T52) $Sp \supset (Wp \ \& \ \sim Cp)$
(T53) $Dp \supset (W \sim p \ \& \ \sim C \sim p)$
(T54) $(\sim Wp \ \& \ \sim W \sim p) \supset (\sim Cp \ \& \ \sim C \sim p)$
(T55) $(Wp \ \& \ \sim W \sim p) \supset \sim C \sim p$
(T56) $(W \sim p \ \& \ \sim Wp) \supset \sim Cp.$

According to (T49), which is the theological reflection of (A6), if God commands something then he wishes for that thing. God commands only what is possible, as (T50) has it, and he does not command the negation of anything necessary, according to (T51). According to (T52) and (T53), if something is supererogatory, then God wishes for it but does not command it, and if something is discreditable, then God wishes for but does not command its negation. We are told by (T54), which reflects (T35), that if a proposition is such that God wishes neither for it nor for its negation to be true, then it is such that God commands neither it nor its negation. According to (T55), if God wishes for something but does not wish for its negation, then he does not command its negation; according to (T56) if God does not wish for something but does wish for its negation, then he does not command that thing. All this seems to be, beyond any reasonable doubt, sound theological doctrine, expressing as it does a kind of coherence between divine wishes and divine commands.

Another possibility which remains open, because we have not postulated (A4), is that both a proposition and its negation should be required. The situation in such a case is summed up by the following theorems:

(T57) $(Rp \ \& \ R \sim p) \equiv (Fp \ \& \ F \sim p)$

(T58) (Fp & F~p) ≡ (~Pp & ~P~p)
(T59) (Rp & R~p) ≡ (~Pp & ~P~p)
(T60) (Cp & C~p) ≡ (Rp & R~p).

It will be recalled that in an earlier chapter we envisaged Abraham being located in such a quandary when confronted with his fateful choice about killing Isaac. Suppose that God commands, in the decalogue, that Abraham does not kill Isaac and God also commands, by direct order, that Abraham kills Isaac. Then, it is required that Abraham kills Isaac and it is required that Abraham does not kill Isaac, according to (T60). In addition, according to (T57), it is forbidden that Abraham kills Isaac and it is forbidden that Abraham does not kill Isaac. Moreover, according to (T58) or (T59), it is not permitted that Abraham kills Isaac, and it is not permitted that Abraham does not kill Isaac. This seems to be an intolerable conclusion, and it appears to be evident that our theory should be strong enough to guarantee that this type of situation will never arise. More precisely, it is clear that we should insist upon postulating the following principle:

(A8) Pp v P~p.

All (A8) asserts is that any proposition is such that either it or its negation is permitted. But this is enough in the context of our other assumptions to allow us to infer some rather strong consequences. Among them are the following:

(T61) ~(~Pp & ~P~p)
(T62) ~(Rp & R~p)
(T63) ~(Fp & F~p)
(T64) Lp ⊃ ~L~p
(T65) Rp ⊃ Pp
(T66) Rp ⊃ ~Fp
(T67) Fp ⊃ ~Rp
(T68) ~(Cp & C~p).

According to (T61), no proposition is such that neither it nor its negation is permitted. We are informed by (T62) that no proposition is such that both it and its negation are required, and (T63) tells us that no proposition is such that both it and its negation are forbidden. According to (T64), which is the deontological counterpart of the notorious (A4), if it is obligatory that p, then it is not obligatory that ~p; though there may be conflict, ultimate and without resolution, in what ought to be the case, no such conflict of obligations is allowed by our theory. We are told by (T65) that whatever is required is also permitted, and (T66) and (T67) together say that the required and the forbidden are mutually exclusive categories. Finally, (T68) assures us that no proposition is such that God commands both it and its negation.

It is worth noting that we can deduce (A8) from (A4) plus some of our other assumptions; hence, (T61)–(T68) would also be theorems if we were to assume (A4). But, in the context of our other assumptions, we cannot deduce (A4) from (A8), and the propositions marked with an asterisk, (T22)–(T30), will not be theorems if we assume (A8) but not (A4). And there are other consequences of (A4) which are not consequences of (A8). Among them are these strengthened versions of (T42) and (T43):

(T69)* $Rp \supset Gp$
(T70)* $Fp \supset Bp$.

There are two possibilities which (A4) closes out but which (A8) leaves open. The first is that there should be some proposition such that both it and its negation ought to be the case and such that either it or its negation (but not both) is required and permitted while the other is forbidden. The second is that there should be some proposition such that both it and its negation ought to be the case and such that both are permitted and neither is required or forbidden. If we wished to rule out the first possibility, it would suffice to assume the following:

(A9)* $(Op \ \& \ O\sim p) \supset \sim(Lp \ v \ L\sim p)$.

However, given our other assumptions, (A9) would have among its theological consequences this doctrine:

(T71)* $(Wp \ \& \ W\sim p) \supset (\sim Cp \ \& \ \sim C\sim p)$.

According to (T71), if a proposition is such that God wishes for it and wishes for its negation, then God does not command it and does not command its negation. This result strikes me as, at best, dubious theology, and so I shall refrain from postulating

(A9). For this reason (A9) and (T71) are marked with asterisks. To rule out the second possibility described above, it would suffice to assume this:

(A10)*   (Op & O∼p) ⊃ (Lp v L∼p).

But (A10) too has a dubious theological consequence, namely, the doctrine according to which:

(T72)*   (Wp & W∼p) ⊃ (Cp v C∼p).

Since I can see no reason for supposing that (T72) expresses a truth, I shall not postulate (A10), and so (A10) and (T72) are also marked with asterisks. And, of course, since (A4) follows from (A9) and (A10) together, it would be unwise for anyone with reservations about (A4) to postulate both (A9) and (A10).

Our official theory, then, will consist of all the definitions, axioms, and theorems we have so far formulated except those marked with asterisks. Excluded from the official theory will be (A4), (A9) and (A10) as well as (T22)–(T30) and (T69)–(T72). Let us rehearse briefly the principal doctrines asserted by our official theory. On the axiological level, the good, the bad, the indifferent, and the extraordinary are mutually exclusive and collectively exhaustive categories. The good and the bad are mirror-images of each other under negation, and each of the indifferent and the extraordinary is its own mirror-image under negation. The impossible is not good, and the necessary is not bad. On the deontological level, the permitted and the forbidden are mutually exclusive and collectively exhaustive categories. The required and the forbidden are mirror-images of each other under negation, and so are the supererogatory and the discreditable. The required is possible, and the necessary is not forbidden. When we mix the two levels, we acquire some additional doctrine. Anything indifferent is such that, with respect to it and its negation, both are permitted, neither is required and neither is forbidden. Anything good is permitted, and nothing bad is required. The required and the forbidden are mutually exclusive and whatever is required is also permitted. No proposition is such that, with respect to it and its negation, neither is permitted, both are required or both are forbidden. Nothing forbidden is good or indifferent, and nothing required is bad or indifferent. If anything is extraordinary, then with respect to it and its negation either one of them is required and permitted and the other is forbidden or both are permitted and neither is required or forbidden. All of this seems to be tenable, indeed plausible, doctrine about the logical relations among ethical concepts. We may conclude, therefore, that our divine command assumptions can be embedded in an ethical framework which, as far as it goes, has some plausibility, scope, and power. Needless to say, our theory might go further than it does now. It was noted above that additional axioms governing iterated occurrences of the O-operator or its interplay with the various sentential connectives could be used to supplement the theory. A similar point can be made about the L-operator. But I shall leave it an open question which, if any, such principles have a ring of self-evidence to them and might thereby merit inclusion in our theory.

What our theory now has to say about the case of Abraham is worth lingering over for a moment. It may be that God wishes that Abraham kills Isaac and wishes that Abraham does not kill Isaac. If this is the case, then the proposition that Abraham kills Isaac falls into the category of the extraordinary, and so does its negation. But God does not command that Abraham kills Isaac and command that Abraham does not kill Isaac. If God does command that Abraham kills Isaac, then it is required that Abraham kills Isaac, and this is permitted and its negation is forbidden. If God commands that Abraham does not kill Isaac, then it is required and permitted that Abraham does not kill Isaac, and it is forbidden that Abraham kills Isaac. If God commands neither of these things, then neither is required or forbidden and both are permitted. But our theory does not tell us which of these three situations confronts Abraham. What is poor Abraham to do? If God commands anything, then Abraham has an obligation to do that thing. If God commands nothing, then Abraham has no obligation but is permitted to choose either course of action, and whatever he does will be in accord with God's wishes in this extraordinary situation. Abraham's problem boils down to finding out whether God has commanded anything and, if so, what he has commanded. Perhaps in the scriptural story he succeeded in discovering what he needed to know, and so it may be that what he did was permitted and something he ought to have done.

More generally, when an agent confronts something in the category we have called 'the extraordinary', then no matter what he does the outcome will be that something which ought to be is not the case. Such a situation, though inevitable, is regrettable, and so it would be appropriate for an agent to feel regret in such circumstances. If we were to omit (A8) and, consequently, (T61)–(T68) from our theory as well, we would allow that situations could arise in which no matter what the agent does something forbidden is the case. We might imagine that an agent trapped in such a situation would incur guilt no matter what he did, for no matter what he does the outcome is one that is morally forbidden and not permitted. This is, I submit, implausible. Are we to say that Antigone becomes guilty when she chooses to bury her brother, or that Nora incurs guilt when she chooses self-realization over wifely subservience? And is Sartre's young man guilty whether he cares for his mother or joins the Resistance? The temptation to think that a proposition and its negation might be such that neither is permitted may arise from thinking of the permitted as the unobjectionable.[3] In the cases of Antigone, Nora, Abraham, and the young Frenchman, neither course of action is unobjectionable. But that does not mean that neither is permitted, for there are circumstances in which it is obligatory and permitted to do objectionable things, as these cases show. And, once we have adopted the view that the permitted and the forbidden are together exclusive and exhaustive categories, we should hesitate before allowing that a proposition and its negation could be such that neither is permitted and both are forbidden. It is not clear that there are, or could be, any cases in which, no matter what an agent does, the outcome is forbidden and the agent incurs guilt. Van Fraassen is certainly correct in insisting that regret and guilt are not the same, but this does not mean that allowing that there may be situations where regret is inevitably appropriate forces us to concede that there are any situations in which guilt is inevitably incurred.[4]

---

[3] Apparently, van Fraassen tends to think in these terms. See ibid., p. 12.
[4] Ibid., p. 14.

What (A8) does, in effect, is to rule out those cases in which an agent would inevitably incur guilt. This is, as I see it, the way things should be in a moral theory.

3

Since the theorems (T46)–(T48) in the theory I have been constructing are consequences of the principles (T1a)–(T1c) which constitute the kernel of what I have earlier described as a simple divine command theory, it would be appropriate to call what we have created 'a simple divine command theory'. For present purposes we may think of the crucial elements of such a theory as being of two kinds. The axiological elements consist of one axiom and four of its consequences:

(A3) $Op \equiv Wp$
(T15) $Gp \equiv (Wp \ \& \ \sim W\sim p)$
(T16) $Bp \equiv (W\sim p \ \& \ \sim Wp)$
(T17) $Ip \equiv (\sim Wp \ \& \ \sim W\sim p)$
(T18) $Ep \equiv (Wp \ \& \ W\sim p)$.

The deontological elements consist of another axiom and three of its consequences:

(A7) $Lp \equiv Cp$
(T46) $Rp \equiv Cp$
(T47) $Fp \equiv C\sim p$
(T48) $Pp \equiv \sim C\sim p$.

Taken together, these nine sentences express the way in which ethical status, both axiological and deontological, depends, according to theory, upon divine wishes and commands.

It is fairly easy to see how we can modify these formulations to produce more complex divine command theories belonging to the family of T2. Such theories should contain non-modal consequences of the kernel assertions expressed by (T2a)–(T2c). Hence, our deontological schema will have the following form:

(A7′) $Lp \equiv (Q(God) \ \& \ Cp)$.

In (A7′) the predicate letter 'Q' is to be replaced by 'is loving', 'creates heaven and earth', 'is almighty' or whatever other actual predicate the divine command theorist thinks will suffice to insure the truth of (A7′). It is evident that this schema will generate a whole family of axioms, a distinct one for each different predicate which is used to replace 'Q'. The corresponding theorems in the more complex theories will have this form:

(T46') $Rp \equiv (Q(God) \& Cp)$
(T47') $Fp \equiv (Q(God \& C{\sim}p)$
(T48') $Pp \equiv {\sim}(Q(God) \& C{\sim}p)$.

These theorem schemata yield the appropriate non-modal consequences of the kernel principles (T2a)–(T2c) of T2 when 'Q' is replaced by 'makes the universe'. Hence, they represent the deontological elements of more complex divine command theories. To simplify the discussion I shall assume that the axiological elements of such complex theories are constructed in the obviously parallel way:

(A3') $Op \equiv (Q(God) \& Wp)$
(T15') $Gp \equiv ((Q(God) \& Wp) \& {\sim}(Q(God) \& W{\sim}p))$
$\equiv (Q(God) \& Wp \& {\sim}W{\sim}p)$
(T16') $Bp \equiv ((Q(God) \& W{\sim}p) \& {\sim}(Q(God) \& Wp))$
$\equiv (Q(God \& W{\sim}p \& {\sim}Wp)$
(T17') $Ip \equiv ({\sim}(Q(God \& Wp) \& {\sim}(Q(God) \& W{\sim}p))$
(T18') $Ep \equiv ((Q(God) \& Wp) \& (Q(God) \& W{\sim}p))$
$\equiv (Q(God) \& Wp \& W{\sim}p)$.

When some instantiations of (A3') and (A7') are substituted for (A3) and (A7) and the appropriate modifications made in the formulations of theorems which depend upon these axioms, the result will be a complex divine command theory. Unfortunately, there is no simple way to incorporate the non-modal consequences of (T3a)–(T3c) and their ilk into the framework of the present discussion, and so I shall ignore theories which have their non-modal consequences as theorems for the remainder of this chapter. Hence, in the present discussion only theories including instantiations of the schemata (A3') and (A7') will be regarded as complex divine command theories.

Let us call the theory which includes (A3), (A7), (T15)–(T18) and (T46)–(T48) along with the other definitions, axioms, and theorems discussed above 'the unprimed theory' or *DCU* for short. And let us call the theories which include instantiations of (A3'), (A7'), (T15')–(T18'), and (T46')–

T48'), along with our other definitions, axioms, and suitably revised theorems 'the primed theories' or *DCP* for short. Neither *DCU* nor any of the *DCP* assert or entail that God exists or that he has any wishes or that he has the various properties attributed to him by the several *DCP* or that he issues any commands. Therefore, in order to get a clear picture of some of the ways in which moral status varies with theological assumption according to these theories we may entertain, hypothetically, the negations of the various things they neither assert nor entail.

Consider first *DCU*. Suppose hypothetically either that God does not exist or that he has no wishes. On this supposition, according to (A3), there is nothing that ought to be the case, and nothing is either good, bad, or extraordinary. Thus, as we can see from (T17), everything is indifferent. Since (T49) tells us that $Cp \supset Wp$, our present supposition has the consequence that there are no divine commands and, hence, that nothing is required or forbidden and everything is permitted. And, as (A7) assures us, in this case there is nothing which is obligatory. These results, coupled with (D9) and (D10), suffice to guarantee that nothing is supererogatory and nothing is discreditable. If we think of the indifferent as that which is outside the moral realm, this assumption has the consequence that everything is outside the moral realm. And, if everything is permitted, then anything goes. Suppose, alternatively, that God exists and has some wishes but issues no commands. On this supposition, nothing is obligatory and, hence, nothing is required or forbidden and everything is permitted. Either there are some things which are good and others which are bad or there are some things which are extraordinary (or both). But everything good is supererogatory and everything bad is merely discreditable because, since everything is permitted, anything goes. This supposition has the curious consequence that the deontological distinctions collapse but the axiological distinctions do not.

Let us next consider the various *DCP*. Suppose first either that God does not exist or that he lacks Q or that he has no wishes. Given this hypothesis, according to (A3'), there is nothing that ought to be the case and, hence, as (T15')–(T18') tell us, nothing is either good, bad, or extraordinary, and everything is indifferent. Moreover, nothing is either super-erogatory or discreditable. The axiological distinctions collapse, and everything is outside the realm of moral value. The appropriate analogues of (T49) are propositions to the effect that $(Q(God)\ \&\ Cp) \supset (Q(God)\ \&\ Wp)$. They do not allow us to infer that there are no divine commands if there are no divine wishes, for something of this form can be true when 'Q(God)' is false, 'Cp' is true and 'Wp' is false. However, if 'Q(God)' is false, then, according to (A7') and (T46')–(T48'), nothing is obligatory, required, or forbidden and everything is permitted. And, if 'Q(God)' is true, then an analogue of (T49) allows us to infer from the premiss that there are no divine wishes the conclusion that there are no divine commands. In this case too, we are assured that nothing is obligatory, required, or forbidden and everything is permitted. Thus, on our present hypothesis, the deontological distinctions collapse too, and because everything is permitted anything goes. Suppose next that God exists, has Q, and has some wishes but issues no commands. This supposition has the same consequences as the parallel second hypothesis about *DCU*. When it is made, we may infer that nothing is obligatory, required or forbidden and everything is permitted, that either there are some good things and some bad things or there are some extraordinary things (or both), and that everything good is supererogatory and everything bad is discreditable. Once again we see a case in which the deontological distinctions but not the axiological distinctions collapse.

We may say, in conclusion, that there are three types of situation which both *DCU* and the several *DCP* allow. In the first type, both axiological and deontological distinctions collapse. Everything is both permitted and indifferent. For *DCU* this occurs if either there is no God or God has no wishes and for the various *DCP* this occurs if either there is no God or God lacks Q or God lacks wishes altogether. Assuming a divine command theory, a situation of the first type amounts to moral nihilism. In the second type, deontological distinctions collapse but axiological distinctions do not. Everything is permitted but either some things are good and others bad or some things are extraordinary. For *DCU* this happens if God exists and has wishes but gives no commands, and for the several *DCP* it happens if God exists and has both Q and wishes but issues no commands. Assuming a divine command theory, a situation of the second type contains moral values but no moral law, that is to say, some things ought to be the case but nothing is obligatory. In the third type, neither set of distinctions collapses. This comes about when God exists, has wishes and gives commands according to *DCU* or when God exists, has Q and wishes and gives commands according to the various *DCP*. As divine command theories have it, situations of the third type contain both moral value and the requirements of moral law because some things ought to be the case and some of them are obligatory. The main point the typology illustrates is the several ways in which, according to our theories, moral status alters in wholesale fashion with changes in theological assumption.

The theory *DCU*, which has been worked out in some detail, and the various theories *DCP*, which could be easily spelt out since they are only variants of *DCU*, have several merits in my opinion. First, they preserve the distinction between value and obligation in the moral realm, between axiology and deontology. Second, they are rich enough to allow us to define a fairly complex network of ethical concepts, including both familiar but occasionally neglected notions such as supererogation and novel but useful ideas such as extraordinariness. Third, they are systematic, precise and orderly as good theories should be. And, fourth, they leave open problems for further thought and research such as the issue of what axioms should govern iterated occurrences of the O- and L-operators. For these reasons I am inclined to take them seriously as theories of the logic of ethical and theological concepts. However, in the context of the present discussion their main function is illustrative. The point they are intended to illustrate is a simple one, namely, that assertions typical of divine command views of ethics can be incorporated without difficulty into ethical frameworks of great conceptual richness and significant precision and power. This seems to me to show conclusively that there are divine command theories which measure up to the best philosophical standards of clarity and precision.

Of course, there are features of moral reasoning which are not captured by the theories we have formulated in this chapter. To

cite only a single example, our logic makes no provision for one
obligation to override another. But, as we shall discover in a
subsequent chapter, logics which do make such provisions can
be supplemented with theological principles which turn them
into divine command theories different from any we have
considered so far but none the less defensible against the
standard philosophical objections.

Finally, a word should be said about the concept of sin. This
concept seems to be properly theological in the sense that non-
religious moral theories can, and usually do, dispense with it.
Abstractly speaking, sin is an offence against God; more
concretely, the sinful is what is contrary to divine commands.
Thus, we are justified in proposing the following definition:

(D11) It is sinful that p = Def C∼p.

In the light of (T47), the sinful and the forbidden coincide
exactly, which is just what one would expect in a divine
command theory. Some philosophers would, I suppose, prefer
to work with a narrower concept of the sinful. For example, it
might be claimed that a person who disobeys a divine command
sins only if he acts with malicious intent or only if he believes he
is disobeying a divine command. According to (D11), however,
a person could sin without intending to do so or without being
aware that he was doing so. This consequence strikes me as
harmless so long as we bear in mind that God might find it
particularly easy to excuse or to forgive such unintentional or
unknowing sins. In any case, I shall have more to say about this
question in the final chapter.

IV

Divine Commands and the Logic of Requirement

WE have already seen how divine commands can be introduced into ethical theories of certain sorts. Such theories have enough resources to allow us to define a large number of ethical concepts. And they can, I have argued, be defended against standard philosophical objections. However, the theories we have studied so far are still impoverished, logically speaking, for they do not permit us to represent all the forms of moral reasoning familiar to us. One important moral phenomenon which is not reflected by these theories is the conflict of requirements and its resolution, or what is sometimes called 'the conflict of duties'. In this chapter I propose to examine a theory which I take to be logically adequate for dealing with conflicting requirements. I shall show how it can be extended so that it is a divine command theory, but a divine command theory rather different from any we have yet studied. Then I shall argue that this theory too can be successfully defended against the standard philosophical criticisms.

I

The purely ethical principles I shall discuss are modelled on a system of general principles set forth by Roderick Chisholm.[1] He calls this system 'the logic of requirement'. My formulation differs from his in one significant respect. Chisholm's ontological posits are states of affairs which are picked out by terms that have the grammatical status of nouns, and his primitive

---

[1] Roderick Chisholm, 'Practical Reason and the Logic of Requirement', *Practical Reason* (ed. Stephen Körner) Oxford: Basil Blackwell (1974), pp. 1–17.

locution is a two-place predicate defined on ordered pairs of nouns which picks out a relation between the states of affairs that are designated by the members of such pairs. By contrast, my ontological commitment will run to propositions which are picked out by things in the grammatical category of declarative sentences, and my primitive locution will be a sentential connective defined on ordered pairs of sentences which picks out a relation between propositions. Because there is an intimate connection, amounting perhaps to an identity, between propositions and states of affairs, this difference is not of much importance. I choose to revise Chisholm's formulations solely for the sake of achieving uniformity of style; since I have been using the usual propositional variables elsewhere, it turns out to be convenient to employ them in my presentation of the logic of requirement too. Apart from this, my treatment differs from Chisholm's only in my having omitted those of his definitions and axioms which contribute nothing to the points I wish to discuss and my addition of theological doctrine to the pure logic of requirement.

Our primitive locution is represented by the expression 'pRq', where the letters 'p' and 'q' may be replaced by declarative sentences. The official reading of this expression will be the following: 'The requirement that q would be imposed if it were the case that p'. Less formally, we may make use of variant readings like these: 'The proposition that p is such that, were it true, it would be required that q', or 'The requirement that q would obtain if it were that p'. It is to be noted that the subjunctive mood is an essential ingredient of our reading of this locution. This means that it is not a truth-functional connective. Also, what would impose a requirement were it the case need not be the case, and so that pRq does not imply that p. A primitive locution is not, of course, to be further clarified by definition, but some additional understanding of the notion of requirement here in question can be gained by attending to some of the general principles which govern it. It will prove convenient to formulate the more fundamental principles as axioms. Deductions of theorems from these axioms will be in accord with the usual rules of inference for propositional calculus and alethic modal logic except that quantification of propositional variables will be allowed.

In order to formulate the first axiom of interest to us we may let 'Mp' stand for 'It is logically possible that p'. Our axiom can then be expressed in this way:

(A1) $pRq \supset M(p \ \& \ q)$.

If one proposition is such that, were it true, it would require another, then the two are compossible. As a consequence of (A1), together with the logical truth that M (p & q) ⊃ Mp, and the symmetry of conjunction and the transitivity of material implication, we readily obtain:

(T1) $pRq \supset Mp$
(T2) $pRq \supset Mq$.

Hence, an impossible proposition would not impose any requirement, and nothing would impose an impossible requirement.

The second axiom we wish to adopt can be expressed in this fashion:

(A2) $(pRq \ \& \ pRs) \supset pR(q \ \& \ s)$.

Any proposition would require the conjunction of all of those propositions such that it would require each of them. From (A1) and (A2) two further theorems of interest can be derived:

(T3) $pRq \supset \sim (pR \sim q)$
(T4) $(pRq \ \& \ sR \sim q) \supset (\sim ((p \ \& \ s)Rq) \ v \ \sim ((p \ \& \ s)R \sim q))$.

A proof for each of these theorems is easy to provide. Obviously, $\sim M (q \ \& \sim q)$. Uniform substitution of 'q & ~q' for 'q' in (T2) yields the result that pR (q & ~q) ⊃ M(q & ~q). Hence, by *modus tollens*, we deduce that $\sim (pR(q \ \& \ \sim q))$. Uniform substitution of '~q' for 's' in (A2) tells us that (pRq & pR ~q) ⊃pR(q & ~q). Using *modus tollens* again, we obtain the result that $\sim (pRq \ \& \ pR \sim q)$. This is tautologically equivalent, by one of DeMorgan's Laws, to the claim that $\sim (pRq) \ v \ \sim (pR \sim q)$, which in turn is tautologically equivalent to (T3). By substituting 'p & s' for 'p' in the penultimate formula of the preceding proof we conclude that $\sim ((p \ \& \ s)Rq) \ v \ \sim ((p \ \& \ s) R \sim q)$. Substituting '$\sim ((p \ \& \ s)Rq) \ v \ \sim ((p \ \& \ s)R \sim q)$' for 'q' and 'pRq & sR ~q' for 'p' in the tautological expression 'q ⊃ (p ⊃q)' and using *modus ponens* we arrive at (T4). What

(T3) tells us is that no proposition, were it true, would impos
contradictory requirements. Thus, if two propositions woul
impose contradictory requirements, then at least one of thes
requirements would not be imposed by their conjunctior
according to (T4). Another way of stating what (T4) asserts i
to say that if two propositions would impose contradictor
requirements, then at least one of these requirements woul
not be imposed, or would be overridden, by the conjunction c
the two propositions.

The concept of overriding is sufficiently important to meri
being enshrined in a separate definition:

(D1) sOpq = Def pRq & ~((p & s) Rq) & M(p & s & q).

The expression 'sOpq' is to be understood as abbreviating th
longer and somewhat awkward expression 'The requiremen
that q which would be imposed if it were the case that p woul
be overridden if it were the case that s.' Another concept whic
will play a major role in our subsequent discussion is picked ou
by this definition:

(D2) pIq = Def pRq & ~(∃s) (sOpq).

The expression 'pIq' is to stand for the expression 'The require
ment that q would be indefeasibly imposed if it were the cas
that p.' If some proposition would indefeasibly impose th
requirement that q, then nothing could override the require
ment that q which would be imposed were that propositio
true.

From the fact that the requirement that q would be impose
if it were the case that p and the additional assumption that p
we may not infer that it is obligatory that q. For there may b
some other proposition such that it is the case and such tha
the requirement that q which would be imposed if it were th
case that p would be overridden if that proposition were th
case. However, even if there is such a proposition, we may no
infer that it is not the case that it is obligatory that q. For ther
may be yet another proposition such that it is the case, th
requirement that q would be imposed if it were the case, and i
entails both the proposition that p and the proposition whic
we supposed to override the requirement imposed by th
proposition that p. Something is obligatory provided there i

a true proposition which imposes the requirement that it be the case and that requirement is not overridden:

(D3) $Oq = \text{Def} \, (\exists p) \, (p \, \& \, pRq \, \& \sim (\exists s) \, (s \, \& \, sOpq))$.

The official reading of 'Oq' is 'It is obligatory that q'; less formally, we may read it as 'It ought to be that q'. In reality, this O-operator is more akin to the L-operator of the previous chapter that to the O-operator of that chapter. In this chapter and the next I use the O-operator to represent obligation; in doing so I gain the benefit of adherence to established notational practice at the risk of obscuring the distinction between what ought to be and what is obligatory. The risk seems small enough to be worth running. We may now define personal obligation in terms of impersonal obligation, as follows:

(D4) x is obligated to do $A = \text{Def} \, O \, (x \text{ does } A)$.

What someone is obligated to do is, on this interpretation, what it is obligatory that he does on balance or in the light of all relevant and actual considerations. Finally, we may define a concept of the supererogatory, slightly different from the one defined in the previous chapter, in this fashion:

(D5) $S(x \text{ brings it about that } q) = \text{Def.} \, Oq \, \& \sim O \, (x \text{ brings it about that } q) \, \& \sim O \sim \\ (x \text{ brings it about that } q)$.

The expression 'Sq' is to be understood as an abbreviation for 'It is supererogatory that q'. What is supererogatory for a given person is what is impersonally obligatory but what he is not obligated to do and not obligated not to do.

Up to this point our discussion of the logic of requirement has made no mention of divine commands or other theological doctrines. What we must do now is supplement this system of definitions and axioms with some assumptions fraught with theological consequences. For this purpose, we may adopt as our primitive theological locution the expression 'Cp', which will be taken to abbreviate 'God commands that p.' Since we must take care to be clear about what propositions this expression designates in the subjunctive context of an R-formula, a word about the way the term 'God' will be used is in order. My practice in this chapter will be to use 'God' as a title. Something merits the title 'God' only if it is a powerful and loving being who is the unique creator of all the contingent things there are. If we assert that CpRp, we are to be understood as saying that the requirement that p would be imposed if it were the case that God, who is the powerful and loving creator, commands that p.

A general principle linking divine commands to moral requirements which should seem plausible to many theists is set forth by the following axiom:

(A3) Mp ⊃ CpIp.

If it is possible that p, then the requirement that p would be indefeasibly imposed if it were the case that God commands that p. Notice that (A3) does not assert or entail that God exists or that, if he does, he issues any commands. In other words, (A3) does not assert that any indefeasible requirement is imposed in virtue of a divine command, only that indefeasible requirements would be imposed if there were divine commands. But neither, to be sure, does (A3) assert or entail that there is no God or that there are no divine commands.

Several theorems of some interest can be proved with the aid of (A3). From (D2) and (T2) we may conclude that CpIp ⊃ Mp. Together with (A3), this result allows us to infer:

(T5) Mp ≡ CpIp.

What (T5) says is that it is possible that p if and only if the requirement that p would be indefeasibly imposed if it were the case that God commands that p. Divine commands could extend exactly as far as logical possibility does. From (A3) and (D2) we may, using the transitivity of material implication, prove two rather obvious theorems:

(T6) Mp ⊃ Cp Rp
(T7) Mp ⊃ ∼(∃s) (sOCpp).

According to (T6), if it is possible that p, then the requirement that p would be imposed if God were to command that p. And, according to (T7), if it is possible that p, then there is no proposition such that the requirement that p which would be imposed if God were to command that p would be overridden if it were the case. These two theorems make explicit, it seems to me, those consequences of our theory which are usually supposed to be most typically asserted by divine command theorists. For instance, since it is all too possible that everyone engages in gratuitous cruelty from time to time, if God were to command that everyone engages in gratuitous cruelty from time to time, then the requirement that everyone engages in gratuitous cruelty from time to time would be imposed, according to (T6), and, moreover, there is nothing such that, if it were the case, that requirement would be overridden, according to (T7).

Another consequence of (A3) tells us what is obligatory if God actually issues commands:

(T8) (Mp & Cp) ⊃ Op.

Since the proof of (T8) is a bit complicated, it may be instructive to see it written out in detail. The justification for each step is indicated on the same line as the step in question:

1.	Mp & Cp	Hypothesis
2.	Mp	1, Conjunction Elimination
3.	Mp ⊃ CpIp	A3
4.	CpIp	2, 3 *Modus Ponens*
5.	CpRp & ~(∃s) (sOCpp)	4, D2
6.	CpRp	5, Conjunction Elimination
7.	~(∃s) (sOCpp)	5, Conjunction Elimination
8.	(∀s)~(sOCpp)	7, Quantifier Interchange
9.	~(sOCpp)	8, Universal Instantiation
10.	~(sOCpp) v~s	9, Disjunction Introduction
11.	~(s & sOCpp)	10, De Morgan's Laws
12.	(∀s)~(s & sOCpp)	11, Universal Generalization
13.	~(∃s) (s & sOCpp)	12, Quantifier Interchange
14.	CpRp & ~(∃s) (s & sOCpp)	5, 13, Conjunction Introduction
15.	Cp	1, Conjunction Elimination
16.	Cp & CpRp & ~(∃s) (s & sOCpp)	14, 15 Conjunction Introduction
17.	(∃q) (q & qRp & ~(∃s) (s & sOqp)	16, Existential Generalization
18.	Op	17, D3
19.	(Mp & Cp) ⊃ Op	1–18, Implication Introduction

What (T8) says is that whatever is possible and commanded

by God is also obligatory. Less exactly, what is possible and divinely commanded ought to be. Surely this is a consequence few orthodox theists would wish to reject. Most theists would, I suppose, also maintain that God has commanded certain things, and so they would be prepared to detach certain instances of the consequent of (T8). But even some atheists might accept (T8). An atheist might, after all, have an elevated conception of God and for that reason accept (T8), even though he would never assert an instance of its antecedent or detach an instance of its consequent.

Another interesting consequence follows directly from (T8). Substituting 'x does A' for 'p' in (T8) and using (D4) and the transitivity of material implication, we obtain:

(T9) (M(x does A) & C (x does A)) ⊃ x is obligated to do A.

What (T9) asserts is that what it is possible that an agent does and is also commanded by God is what an agent is obligated to do. So, for instance, if God commands that Dr. Kildare plays golf on Wednesdays, then Dr. Kildare is obliged to play golf on Wednesdays. This is, needless to say, a very strong claim because what is logically possible may not be physically possible or within the power of a given agent. It is, I imagine, logically possible that I travel to the moon in less than a minute, and so if God commands that I do so then I am obliged to do so. Nevertheless, it is clear that I lack the power to perform this feat and thus am unable to do so. Theists may, of course, trust that God never commands anyone to do anything which he is unable to do, but the possibility that this might happen is not ruled out by our theory.

We are now in a position to see how our theory deals with conflicts between ordinary moral requirements and those imposed by divine fiat. In order to be specific, let us consider once again the situation of Abraham. Evidently it is possible that Abraham kills Isaac. We may assume, I think, that the requirement that Abraham does not kill Isaac would be imposed if it were the case that Isaac is an innocent child. Since Isaac is an innocent child, the requirement that Abraham does not kill Isaac is imposed, we may say, by the fact that Isaac is an innocent child. However, because it is possible that Abraham kills Isaac, (T6) informs us that the requirement that

Abraham kills Isaac would be imposed if God were to command that Abraham kills Isaac. Here we have a clear case of conflict in what would be required. According to (T4), either it is not the case that the requirement that Abraham kills Isaac would be imposed if it were the case both that God commands that Abraham kills Isaac and that Isaac is an innocent child, or it is not the case that the requirement that Abraham does not kill Isaac would be imposed if it were the case both that God commands that Abraham kills Isaac and that Isaac is an innocent child. But which of these two requirements would be overridden in these circumstances? According to (T7), either it is not the case that the requirement that Abraham kills Isaac would be imposed if God were to command that Abraham kills Isaac, or the requirement that Abraham kills Isaac would be imposed if it were the case both that God commands that Abraham kills Isaac and that Isaac is an innocent child, or it is not possible that Isaac is an innocent child and that God commands that Abraham kills Isaac and that Abraham kills Isaac. But it is the case that the requirement that Abraham kills Isaac would be imposed if God were to command that Abraham kills Isaac, and it is possible that Isaac is an innocent child, that God commands that Abraham kills Isaac and that Abraham kills Isaac. Hence, by two applications of the rule of Disjunctive Syllogism, the requirement that Abraham kills Isaac would be imposed if it were the case both that God commands that Abraham kills Isaac and that Isaac is an innocent child. Therefore, it is not the case that the requirement that Abraham does not kill Isaac would be imposed if it were the case both that God commands that Abraham kills Isaac and that Isaac is an innocent child. In brief, though the requirement that Abraham does not kill Isaac is imposed by the fact that Isaac is an innocent child, that requirement would be overridden if, in addition, God were to command that Abraham kills Isaac. If Judaeo-Christian theists who take Scripture literally are correct, God does command that Abraham kills Isaac. If this is so, then the requirement that Abraham kills Isaac is imposed by the facts that God commands that Abraham kills Isaac and that Isaac is an innocent child. Since this requirement, if imposed, would be indefeasibly imposed, if it is imposed, it is indefeasibly imposed. According to our present theory, therefore, Abraham operates under no mysterious 'teleological suspension of the ethical'; instead, he operates under an indefeasibly imposed requirement. And, it goes without saying, parallel arguments will be appropriate whenever a requirement which would be imposed by a divine command comes into conflict with a requirement which would be imposed by something other than a divine command.

But what are we to say about a case in which there are conflicting requirements each of which would be imposed by a divine command? At first blush it would seem that such cases might arise because it seems to be possible both that God commands that p and that God commands that $\sim$p. Perhaps only an inattentive god would fall into such a muddle, but the possibility of such a conflict is interesting none the less. In order to deal with this situation, we may make one additional theological assumption. It seems plausible to suppose, if only for reasons of symmetry, the following principle:

(A4) $(Cp \ \& \ C\sim p) \ Rp \equiv (Cp \ \& \ C\sim p) \ R\sim p.$

Two theorems which will help to answer our query can be deduced with the aid of (A4). They are the following:

(T10) $\sim((Cp \ \& \ C\sim p) \ Rp)$
(T11) $\sim((Cp \ \& \ C\sim p) \ R\sim p).$

Proofs for these theorems can be set forth in this fashion:

1.	$(Cp \ \& \ C\sim p) \ Rp \equiv (Cp \& \ C\sim p) \ R\sim p$	A4
2.	$((Cp \ \& \ C\sim p) \ Rp \ \& \ (Cp \ \& \ C\sim p) \ R\sim p)$ $v \ (\sim((Cp \ \& \ C\sim p) \ Rp) \ \& \ \sim$ $((Cp \ \& \ C\sim p) \ R\sim p))$	1, Tautology
3.	$((Cp \ \& \ C\sim p) \ Rp \ \& \ (Cp \ \& \ C\sim p)$ $R\sim p) \supset (Cp \ \& \ C\sim p) \ R \ (p \ \& \sim p)$	A2
4.	$(Cp \ \& \ C\sim p) \ R \ (p \ \& \sim p) \supset M(p \ \& \sim p)$	T2
5.	$\sim M(p \ \& \sim p)$	Logical Truth
6.	$\sim((Cp \ \& \ C\sim p) \ R \ (p \ \& \sim p))$	4, 5, *Modus Tollens*
7.	$\sim((Cp \ \& \ C\sim p) \ Rp \ \& \ (Cp \ \& \ C\sim p)$ $R\sim p)$	3, 6, *Modus Tollens*
8.	$\sim((Cp \ \& \ C\sim p) \ Rp) \ \& \ \sim((Cp \ \& \ C\sim p)$ $R\sim p)$	2, 7 Disj.Syl.
9.	$\sim((Cp \ \& \ C\sim p) \ Rp)$	8, Conj. Elim.
10.	$\sim((Cp \ \& \ C\sim p) \ R\sim p)$	8, Conj. Elim.

According to (T10), it is not the case that the requirement that p would be imposed if it were the case both that God commands that p and that God commands that ~p. And (T11) tells us that the requirement that ~p would not be imposed in these circumstances either. In other words, if God were to command each of two contradictory propositions, neither would be obligatory. How do these results square with our assertion that divine commands would impose indefeasible requirements? The following sequence of theorems provides an answer to this question:

(T12) Mp ⊃ ~M(Cp & C~p & p)

Proof:

1. Mp	Hypothesis
2. CpIp	1, A3, *Modus Ponens*
3. CpRp & ~(∃s) (sOCpp)	2, D2
4. CpRp	3, Conj. Elim.
5. ~(∃s) (sOCpp)	3, Conj. Elim.
6. (∀s) ~(sOCpp)	5, Quantifier Interchange
7. (∀s) ~(CpRp & ~((s & Cp)Rp) & M(s & Cp & p))	6, D1
8. (∀s) (~CpRp v (s & Cp) Rp v ~M(s & Cp & p))	7, De Morgan's Laws
9. ~CpRp v (Cp & C~p) Rp v ~M(Cp & C~p & p))	8, Universal Instantiation
10. (Cp & C~p) Rp v ~M(Cp & C~p & p)	4, 9, Disj. Syl.
11. ~M(Cp & C~p & p)	10, T10, Disj. Syl.
12. Mp ⊃ ~M(Cp & C~p & p)	1–11, Implication Introduction

(T13) M~p ⊃ ~M(Cp & C~p & ~p).

Proof: Parallel to the proof of (T12) with '~p' replacing 'p', 'C~p' replacing 'Cp', and 'Cp' instead of 'C~p' being instantiated for 's' at the ninth step.

(T14) (Mp & ~M~p) ⊃ ~M (Cp & C~p).

Proof:

1. Mp & ~M~p	Hypothesis
2. Mp	1, Conj. Elim.
3. ~M(Cp & C~p & p)	2, T12, *Modus Ponens*

4. N~(Cp & C~p & p)	3, Logical Equivalence
5. N(~(Cp & C~p) v ~p)	4, De Morgan's Laws
6. N(p ⊃ ~(Cp & C~p))	5, Tautology
7. Np ⊃ N~(Cp & C~p)	6, Logical Truth
8. ~M~p	1, Conj. Elim.
9. Np	8, Logical Equivalence
10. N~(Cp & C~p)	7, 9, *Modus Ponens*
11. ~M(Cp & C~p)	10, Logical Equivalence
12. (Mp & ~M~p) ⊃ ~M (Cp & C~p)	1–11, Implication Introduction

The expression 'Np' abbreviates 'It is necessary that p'. It is introduced by means of the usual definition: Np = Def ~ M ~ p.

(T15) (Mp & M~p) ⊃ ~M(Cp & C~p).

Proof:

1. Mp & M~p	Hypothesis
2. Mp	1, Conj. Elim.
3. M~p	1, Conj. Elim.
4. ~M(Cp & C~p & p)	2, T12, *Modus Ponens*
5. ~M(Cp & C~p & ~p)	3, T13, *Modus Ponens*
6. ~M(Cp & C~p & p) & ~M(Cp & C~p & ~p)	4, 5, Conj. Intro.
7. ~M((Cp & C~p & p) v (Cp & C~p & ~p))	6, Logical Equivalence
8. ~M(Cp & C~p & (pv~p))	7, Distribution
9. N~(Cp & C~p & (p v ~p))	8, Logical Equivalence
10. N(~(Cp & C~p) v ~(p v ~p))	9, De Morgan's Laws
11. N((p v ~p) ⊃ ~(Cp & C~p))	10, Tautology
12. N(p v ~p) ⊃ N~(Cp & C~p)	11, Logical Truth
13. N(p v ~p)	Logical Truth
14. N~(Cp & C~p)	12, 13, *Modus Ponens*
15. ~M(Cp & C~p)	14, Logical Equivalence
16. (Mp & M~p) ⊃ ~M(Cp & C~p)	1–15, Implication Introduction

(T16) Mp ⊃ ~M(Cp & C~p).

Proof:

1. (~M~p & Mp) ⊃ ~M(Cp & C~p)	T14
2. (M~p & Mp) ⊃ ~M(Cp & C~p)	T15

3. $\sim M \sim p \supset (Mp \supset \sim M(Cp \ \& \ C \sim p))$ 1, Exportation

4. $M \sim p \supset (Mp \supset \sim M(Cp \ \& \ C \sim p))$ 2, Exportation

5. $(M \sim p \lor \sim M \sim p) \supset (Mp \supset \sim M(Cp \ \& \ C \sim p))$ 3, 4, Tautology

6. $M \sim p \ \lor \ \sim M \sim p$ Excluded Middle

7. $Mp \supset \sim M(Cp \ \& \ C \sim p)$ 5, 6, *Modus Ponens*

The situation with respect to seeming conflicts among divine commands is now easily summarized. Suppose, first, that Mp & $\sim M \sim p$. On this supposition, (A3) tells us that CpIp, and from (D2) we may infer that CpRp. However, (T5) tells us that $\sim (C \sim pI \sim p)$, and from (T2) we may infer that $\sim (C \sim pR \sim p)$. If the proposition that p is necessary, then the requirement that p would be imposed if God were to command that p but the requirement that $\sim p$ would not be imposed if God were to command that $\sim p$. Moreover, (T10) and (T11) inform us that $\sim ((Cp \ \& \ C \sim p)Rp)$ and $\sim ((Cp \ \& \ C \sim p)R \sim p)$. This does not mean that the requirement that p which would be imposed if Cp would be overridden if $C \sim p$. Rather, since (T12) tells us that $\sim M(Cp \ \& \ C \sim p \ \& \ p)$, (D1) informs us that $\sim (C \sim pOCpp)$. The reason why $\sim ((Cp \ \& C \sim p)Rp)$ is that $\sim M(Cp \ \& \ C \sim p)$, as (T14) informs us. Suppose, next, that Mp & $M \sim p$. On this supposition, (A3) tells us both that CpIp and $C \sim pI \sim p$, and hence (D2) allows us to infer that CpRp and that $C \sim pR \sim p$. If the proposition that p is possible but not necessary, then the requirement that p would be imposed if God were to command that p and the requirement that $\sim p$ would be imposed if God were to command that $\sim p$. However, (T10) and (T11) tell us that $\sim ((Cp \ \& \ C \sim p)Rp)$ and $\sim ((Cp \ \& \ C \sim p)R \sim p)$. This does not mean that the requirement that p which would be imposed if Cp would be overriden if $C \sim p$, nor does it mean that the requirement that $\sim p$ which would be imposed if $C \sim p$ would be overridden if Cp. Since (T12) tells us that $\sim M(Cp \ \& \ C \sim p \ \& \ p)$, (D1) informs us that $\sim (C \sim pOCpp)$, and because (T13) tells us that $\sim M(Cp \ \& \ C \sim p \ \& \ \sim p)$, (D1) informs us that $\sim (CpOC \sim p \sim p)$. Instead, the reason why both $\sim ((Cp \ \& \ C \sim p)Rp)$ and $\sim ((Cp \ \& \ C \sim p)R \sim p)$ is that $\sim M(Cp \ \& \ C \sim p)$, as (T15) assures us.

These results create a problem for Judaeo-Christian theists who might wish to adopt our theory. If they take Scripture literally, they may want to say that, in promulgating the decalogue, God commanded, at least implicitly, that Abraham does not kill Isaac but also that God commanded by some sort of direct revelation that Abraham kills Isaac. But (T16) assures us that this cannot be the case, and so according to our theory such theists cannot have their cake and eat it too. Since it is possible that Abraham kills Isaac, according to (T9), if God did command that Abraham kills Isaac, Abraham is obliged to kill Isaac, but according to (T16), if God so commanded, then God did not command that Abraham does not kill Isaac. And, since it is equally possible that Abraham does not kill Isaac, according to (T9), if God did command that Abraham does not kill Isaac, then Abraham is obliged not to kill Isaac, but according to (T16), if God so commanded, then God did not command that Abraham kills Isaac. If God commands either of these things, there is no problem about what Abraham ought to do; he is obliged to do whichever thing he has been divinely commanded to do. Abraham's problem is only epistemic. How does he learn which of the two courses of action, if either, has in fact been commanded by God? A Judaeo-Christian theist reflecting on these matters must also confront a problem if he adheres to our theory. His is hermeneutical. Which scriptural text is he to decline to take literally? Those who maintain that the decalogue's prohibition on killing covers the case of Abraham and Isaac cannot also claim that God commanded Abraham to kill Isaac if they are to remain consistent with our theory. But, of course, there are edifying lessons which can be drawn from various merely symbolical readings of the story of Abraham and Isaac. Perhaps, for example, the significance of the story is only that God finds burnt animal offerings an acceptable substitute for human sacrifice. By contrast, those who claim that God did command that Abraham kills Isaac cannot also maintain, while remaining consistent with our theory, that the decalogue's prohibition on killing extends to the case of Abraham and Isaac. Since religious casuists defend other exceptions to that prohibition— for example, killing in self-defence—they can also, I would think, defend an exception in this case. Perhaps they may wish to interpret the prohibition as saying: 'Thou shalt not kill unless I, Yahweh, tell you otherwise!' A dangerous doctrine, no doubt, but one consistent with both our theory and a literal reading of the story of Abraham and Isaac. There are solutions aplenty to the problem to which we have drawn attention; all that our theory precludes is the kind of strict and comprehensive fundamentalism which would take literally both texts which together generate a conflict among divine commands.

A salient feature of our theory, and one worth emphasizing a bit, is its weakness in comparison with the theories discussed in previous chapters. In effect, all that (A3) asserts is that divine commands, were they to occur, would be sufficient to impose indefeasible requirements. And what (T8) asserts is that if it is possible that p, then a divine command that p is a sufficient condition for the claim that it is obligatory that p. Our theory does not assert or entail that divine commands would be necessary to impose requirements, nor does it assert or entail that divine commands would not be necessary to impose requirements. Moreover, it does not assert or entail that divine commands are necessary conditions for what is obligatory or what one is obliged to do, nor does it assert or entail that divine commands are not necessary conditions for such things. On all these questions, our theory stands mute; it underdetermines, by a long shot, the doctrine to be held about such matters.

One consequence of this weakness is that our theory does not permit us to derive anything analogous to the Karamazov Thesis. That thesis, it will be recalled, is the claim:

If there were no God, everything would be permitted.

But it is easy to see that no claim this strong is a consequence of our theory. Consider, for the sake of definiteness, our obligation to honour our parents. Our theory has it that the requirement that we honour our parents would be imposed if God were to command that we honour our parents, and indefeasibly so. Presumably, Judaeo-Christian theists also believe that God has commanded that we honour our parents. So they ought to hold, if they accept our theory, that the requirement that we honour our parents is imposed, and indefeasibly so, by the fact that God has commanded that we honour our parents. However, it is consistent with all of this to maintain also that there is something else which would, if it were the case, impose the requirement that we honour our parents. It seems plausible to suppose, for example, that the requirement that we honour our parents would be imposed if our parents were to care for us in the tender years of youth. Undoubtedly, since some of our parents have done just this, the requirement that certain people honour their parents is imposed by the fact that their parents have cared for them in the years of their youth. Assuming further, as we may consistently do, that this requirement is in some cases at least not overridden, we may conclude that in such cases, even if there were no God, those people are obliged to honour their parents. It would not be morally permitted for them not to honour their parents. In short, even if there were no God and, hence, the requirements which would be imposed by divine commands were not imposed by divine commands, still some requirements, perhaps even some of the same requirements which would be imposed by divine commands, might be such that they would be imposed by something else or even are imposed by something else. With reference to the actual world, it is even clearer that it is consistent with our theory to suppose that there is no God but yet that certain things are obligatory, for there are instances of the claim that $M(((Cp \mathbin{\&} Mp) \supset Op) \mathbin{\&} {\sim}Cp \mathbin{\&} Mp \mathbin{\&} Op)$ which seem to be obviously true. For example, surely it is possible that, if God commands that Ford pardons Nixon and it is possible that Ford pardons Nixon, then it is obligatory that Ford pardons Nixon, and that God does not command that Ford pardons Nixon but that it is possible that Ford pardons Nixon and that it is obligatory that Ford pardons Nixon. Therefore, the supposition that there is no God does not have as a consequence the collapse of moral distinctions or the breakdown of the moral concepts embedded in our theory.

Our present theory is a strange creature. On the one hand, it captures many of the data which traditional divine command theorists have wished to insist upon. For example, all of the following claims can be derived very simply from (A3), as should be immediately apparent:

If God were to command that Smith tortures young children for his own amusement, then the requirement that Smith tortures young children for his own amusement would be imposed (and indefeasibly so).

If God were to command that Harris does not eat chocolate ice cream, then the requirement that Harris does not each chocolate ice-cream would be imposed (and indefeasibly so).

If God were to command that everyone refrains from performing abortions, then the requirement that everyone refrains from performing abortions would be imposed (and indefeasibly so).

If God were to command that no one eats meat, then the requirement that no one eats meat would be imposed (and indefeasibly so).

But, on the other hand, it does not have the Karamazov Thesis, or other claims about the collapse of moral distinctions or the inapplicability of moral concepts in a godless world, as consequences. Perhaps the combination of these two features enhances its plausibility or makes it more palatable to those who would otherwise have no taste for divine command theories. What is of more concern to us, since we are engaged in investigating the defensibility of divine command theories, is how well it stands up to the standard philosophical objections. We may now, I believe, profitably turn our attention to this topic.

2

Let us call the theory we have been formulating 'the theological version of the logic of requirement' or *LRT* for short. In defending *LRT* against the standard objections, we will often cover much the same ground as we did in defending the modal kernels of *DCU* and the various *DCP*; when this happens, our discussion can be mercifully brief. On some points, however, *LRT* raises problems we have not confronted before, and in those cases we shall have to proceed cautiously.

The claim that *LRT* tries but fails to define its ethical vocabulary in terms of its theological vocabulary is quite evidently false. All the pieces of ethical vocabulary in *LRT* are defined in terms of a single primitive ethical locution independent of, and in our formulation prior to, the introduction of any piece of theological vocabulary. The theological axiom (A3) does not even have the proper form for a definition; it is a conditional rather than a biconditional. Moreover, though our theological axiom (A4) is a biconditional, it is a postulate within our theory and would be obviously circular if it were mistaken for a definition. Hence, *LRT* can be seen by inspection not to be a theory about the meaning of certain ethical terms and should not be so understood. Neither should *LRT* be interpreted as an attempt to provide a theological analysis of some ethical concepts. In so far as *LRT* contains anything that might be plausibly thought of as analysis, it is embodied in (D1)–(D5) which provide analyses of some complex ethical notions in terms of the concept singled out by the undefined expression 'pRq'. The theological axiom (A3) is obviously not an analysis of any ethical concept because it does not have the proper logical form for an analysis, and our theological axiom (A4) could not provide a theological analysis of our primitive ethical locution because that locution appears on both sides of the biconditional.

There are, however, epistemic asymmetries generated by the fact that *LRT* specifies conditions which are sufficient, or would be, but does not give conditions that are necessary, or would be, for requirements to be imposed. Thus, to focus on a simple case, someone might come to know that something possible is obligatory by first learning that God has commanded it and then inferring from (T8) that it is obligatory. But (T8) cannot be used to infer the absence of moral obligations from the absence of divine commands, for such an inference would involve the fallacy of denying the antecedent. Similarly, someone might come to know that something possible is not commanded by God by first learning that the thing in question is not obligatory, yet one cannot infer from the premiss that something is obligatory the conclusion that something is commanded by God without fallaciously affirming the consequent of (T8). But these asymmetries, far from constituting objections to *LRT*, are consequences of an asymmetry which inheres in the logical structure of that theory. Hence, asymmetries such as those just mentioned, as well as similar ones cast in the subjunctive mood, do not serve to refute or undermine *LRT*.

The reply to the charge that *LRT* underwrites fallacious inferences from is-statements about what is possible and divinely commanded to ought-statements about what is obligatory remains the same as in our previous discussion. Such inferences rely, at least tacitly, upon (T8) and are formally valid, and thus are not fallacies of formal logic. Of course, such arguments will be unsound if (T8) expresses something false, but something beyond the mere assertion that they are unsound would be needed to refute (T8) without begging the question against *LRT*.

The objections suggested by what Socrates says in the *Euthyphro* can be recast in terms of the concepts of *LRT* without any difficulty. The crucial claims, formulated in terms of causes and reasons respectively, may be put in the following way:

It is not the case that God's commanding that p would bring it about that the requirement that p would be indefeasibly imposed.

It is not the case that God's commanding that p would be the reason that the requirement that p would be indefeasibly imposed.

So stated, these counter-claims are usefully thought of as objections to (A3), provided we restrict our attention to the realm of the possible. And, needless to say, someone who wishes to defend the claim that (A3) makes can consistently deny either or both of these dogmas, for it does not appear to be evident that either of them is true. Would such denials have any odour of plausibility? I think they would. After all, if God, who would be the powerful and loving creator of all contingent beings if he were to exist, were to command something, then surely that would suffice to bring about the indefeasible imposition of a requirement for that thing. Similarly, if God, the powerful and loving creator of us all, were to command something, then quite clearly that would be a sufficient reason why a requirement for that thing would be indefeasibly imposed. Or, at least, it seems to me that a defender of (A3) can make these claims with no less plausibility than his partner in disputation urges their negations. Since, in the context of the present discussion, 'God' is being used as a title which only the powerful and loving creator would merit, the objections are at best inconclusive for the same reasons that analogous claims failed earlier to refute the complex versions of the kernel assertions of divine command theories.

All the axioms and other theorems of *LRT* are conditional in character, having the form of explicit indicative conditionals expressed in terms of material implication or of implicit subjunctive conditionals couched in terms of our primitive and defined ethical locutions. For this reason *LRT*, by itself, prescribes nothing outright. To generate actual prescriptions *LRT* would have to be supplemented with some substantive theological assumptions specifying what God has commanded or what requirements are imposed by certain non-theological propositions. However, given such auxiliary assumptions, genuine prescriptions could be derived from *LRT* by means of formally valid arguments, and this suffices to show that the ethical terms in *LRT* have their normal prescriptive force in the sense that they express concepts which in certain contexts of use do function to prescribe. The ethical terms embedded in *LRT* are, as it were, potentially prescriptive because without ambiguity or equivocation they become actual instruments for prescription once certain auxiliary hypotheses are added to *LRT*. Therefore, we may say that the ethical vocabulary of *LRT* lacks none of its usual prescriptive force; that vocabulary is as apt for prescribing in the context of *LRT* as it is in any moral theory.

Universalizability constitutes no problem for *LRT*. Since (A3) and those of its consequences with theological import are, with respect to the propositional variables ingredient in them, explicitly general, this is particularly obvious. Anything possible and commanded by God would be indefeasibly required; so any two things possible and commanded by God, no matter what their other points of similarity and difference, are equally required in an indefeasible way. Therefore, universalizability with respect to the property of having been commanded by God is built into *LRT*, though that theory does not preclude universalizability in other respects since divine commands are not asserted to be necessary for the imposition of requirements. For essentially the same reason *LRT* does not give rise to a trivial natural theology. We may not infer that there is a God from the undeniable fact that there are moral requirements and obligations. *LRT* asserts that the existence of a God who gives orders is sufficient for the imposition of requirements but does not assert that this condition is also necessary; hence, for all that *LRT* explicitly claims there may be other conditions, and non-theological ones at that, which also suffice to impose requirements and obligations. Because this possibility is not ruled out, the fact that there are requirements and obligations implies only that some sufficient condition for their imposition obtains and does not imply that there is a God who has issued commands to his human creatures.

It is hard to see just how moral intuitions are to be deployed in criticism of *LRT*. Since that theory does not assert that every obligation is imposed by divine fiat, but only that every divine command imposes an obligation, it allows for agreement between secular and religious moralists about requirements imposed by things other than divine commands. Indeed, *LRT* even allows that requirements may be over-determined. Hence, it could happen that both a divine command and something else would impose a certain requirement. A religious moralist might claim, for instance, that the requirement that we feed the hungry is imposed indefeasibly by a divine command, while a secular moralist insists that the requirement in question is imposed by the fact that hungry people suffer. It is consistent with *LRT* to suppose that both claims are correct, and so up to this point moral intuitions seem to have no leverage against the claims of *LRT*. As was the case with our other theories, the disputed territory lies beyond the realm of the actual in certain hypothetical and presumably counterfactual circumstances. The proponent of *LRT* is committed to claims of the following sort:

If God, the powerful and loving creator, were to command that people perform acts of gratuitous cruelty, then the requirement that people perform acts of gratuitous cruelty would be indefeasibly imposed.

No doubt there are moralists who would reject this contention with a sputter of outrage. What is not so clear is whether their intuitions suffice to settle the question of its truth value. We would expect the circumstances under which a powerful and loving creator would command gratuitous cruelty to be very unusual ones, though perhaps it would be difficult to say just how they would differ from the circumstances that actually obtain. Intuition, which has been tutored by actuality, might prove an unreliable guide to figuring out what would be required of us in such circumstances. And so a proponent of *LRT* need not acknowledge that the intuitions of someone who denies that a divine command of gratuitous cruelty would impose a requirement to that effect are a decisive refutation of his theory.

Practical objections to *LRT* appear to be particularly weak. In the first place, a person who held *LRT* and denied that there were any divine commands would not be forced to conclude that there are no requirements or that nothing is obligatory. He might maintain that there are other things which would, even in the absence of divine commands, suffice to impose requirements and that some obligations are generated in this way. Thus, an atheist who adhered to *LRT* would not be forced by logic alone into that variety of moral libertinism according to which nothing is obligatory and everything is permitted. In the second place, accepting *LRT* need not increase the risk of widespread moral scepticism or social chaos. To be sure, there are many people who will never honestly be able to regard *LRT* with anything but profound scepticism. But since *LRT* allows that circumstances other than divine commands may be such that they would impose requirements, someone who accepts *LRT* and someone who does not could agree to a very great extent about which things are in fact obligatory. Perhaps the area of agreement would be large enough to lay the basis for social harmony between religious and non-religious people. Of course, *LRT* also provides a framework for profound disagreement about cases such as that of Abraham. Many moral theorists would maintain that under no circumstances would a requirement that Abraham kills Isaac be imposed, but a proponent of *LRT* would have to claim that it would be obligatory that Abraham kills Isaac if God were to command this. But conflict of opinion about such rare cases does not seem likely to disrupt whatever consensus there may be about ordinary moral requirements. However, the potential for conflict which might lead to social tension remains. A liberal secular moralist can afford to reject out of hand claims by religious inquisitors to be doing what is required of them and to dismiss inquisitors as religious fanatics. But within *LRT* one must admit that the inquisitors, if they are really acting in obedience to divine commands, are doing what they are obliged to do, and so in this context, in order to reject the inquisitors' claims with reason, one must provide reasons for thinking that they are not acting in obedience to genuine divine commands. Such an issue might be a point of social disruption; it once was and could become so again. However, moral disagreements about such issues as extra-marital sex and abortion, which sometimes have religious roots, strain the social fabric without tearing it apart, and it does not seem likely that *LRT*, even if widely held, would increase such tensions to the point where they would become intolerable. And so the critic's charge that widespread belief in *LRT* would be bound to lead to moral scepticism or social chaos has not been proven. Such an outcome is, admittedly, possible but has not been shown to be at all likely or to be inevitable.

Briefly, then, the standard objections do not serve to refute *LRT* conclusively. Indeed, in virtue of the fact that *LRT* has one-way conditionals expressing the dependency of requirements and obligations on divine commands where other theories have biconditionals or even logical equivalences, *LRT* fares better in the face of these objections than do stronger theories. At the very least *LRT* is a defensible theory of moral obligation; hence, it is a philosophically interesting theological extension of the logic of requirement.

As a bonus, we have in *LRT* the resources to define the distinction between *prima facie* duties and actual duties often employed in philosophical discussion. The appropriate distinction is captured by these two definitions:

(D6) x has a *prima facie* duty to do A = Def ($\exists$p) (p & pR (x does A)).

(D7) x has an actual duty to do A = Def x is obligated to do A.

A *prima facie* duty is one that may be overridden as circumstances pile up, but an actual duty is one that will never in fact be overridden. Given the assumptions of *LRT*, we may say that duties imposed by divine commands are always actual duties and never merely *prima facie* duties.

V

Divine Commands and Deontic Logics

DEONTIC logics are best conceived as formal systems designed to capture the logical principles which govern reasoning involving what ought to be. Sometimes what ought to be is thought of, narrowly, as encompassing no more than the obligatory; other deontic logicians take what ought to be as covering, broadly, whatever is ideal, good, or valuable. In either case, the strategy for constructing a system of deontic logic consists of formulating principles regulating the use of either a concept of unconditional oughtness, often expressed by the locution 'Op' or 'It ought to be that p', or a concept of conditional oughtness, usually expressed by the locution 'O (p/q)' or 'Given that q, it ought to be that p.' Though serious work on the subject is of recent vintage, the enterprise has become formidably technical as logicians have applied sophisticated techniques of proven value in other areas of modal logic to research problems in deontic logic. It is not my purpose to report the technical details of the most recent work in the field. Instead, I am interested in discovering whether the fundamental conceptions of some of the more intriguing systems of deontic logic are compatible with a divine command conception of what ought to be. What I shall argue for in this chapter is the claim that several of these systems of deontic logic can be provided with foundations in a divine command conception of what ought to be.

I

The most direct way to get at some of the issues which arise when one attempts to construct a deontic logic is to examine with some care an elementary logical theory which deals with the concept of what ought to be unconditionally. Let us begin by assuming that propositional calculus is our basic or underlying logic. To the grammatical resources of propositional calculus we add the primitive locution 'Op' which is to be read as 'It ought to be that p'. The well-formed formulas of what may be called 'Standard Deontic Logic', or *SDL* for short, can be specified in the following way: (1) If p is a well-formed formula of propositional calculus, then Op is a well-formed formula of *SDL*; (2) Any truth-function of well-formed formulas of *SDL* is also a well-formed formula of *SDL*; and (3) Nothing else is a well-formed formula of *SDL*.[1] In effect, the well-formed formulas of *SDL* consist of only well-formed formulas of propositional calculus prefixed by a single O-operator and truth-functions of such formulas as these. Mixed formulas such as 'p v Op' and iterated occurrences of the O-operator as in 'OOp' are not within the expressive power of *SDL*. This is, quite obviously, a drastic simplification, but, as we shall see, many important philosophical problems can be raised even within the confines of this austere grammar.

Next we must specify the axiomatic base of *SDL*. Any formula derived from a tautology of propositional calculus by uniform substitution of formulas of *SDL* for all propositional variables is an axiom of *SDL*. In addition, the following principles, proposed by von Wright, are axioms of *SDL*:

(A1) $O(p \mathbin{\&} q) \supset (Op \mathbin{\&} Oq)$
(A2) $(Op \mathbin{\&} Oq) \supset O(p \mathbin{\&} q)$
(A3) $\sim Of$

where 'f' is a propositional constant which stands for an arbitrarily selected contradiction of propositional calculus.[2] Our rules of inference will be these: (1) a rule of *modus ponens* or detachment according to which if it is provable that $p \supset q$ and also that p, then it is provable that q; (2) a rule of uniform substitution; and (3) a rule of replacement according to which tautologically equivalent formulas may replace one another in

---

[1] I have taken this version of Standard Deontic Logic from Bengt Hansson, 'An Analysis of Some Deontic Logics', *Nous* 3 (1969), pp. 373–98.
[2] G. H. von Wright proposed these axioms in 'Deontic Logic', *Mind* 60 (1951), pp. 1–15.

any formula of *SDL*. From these axioms and rules we are able to deduce the following theorems:

(T1) $Op \supset \sim O \sim p$
(T2) $(O(p \supset q) \, \& \, Op) \supset Oq.$

The proof of (T1) goes as follows: Substitution in (A2) yields the result that $(Op \, \& \, O \sim p) \supset O(p \, \& \, \sim p)$; since all contradictions are equivalent replacement applied to (A3) tells us that $\sim O(p \, \& \, \sim p)$; by the use of *modus tollens* we obtain the result that $\sim (Op \, \& \, O \sim p)$, which is tautologically equivalent to the conclusion that $Op \supset \sim O \sim p$. The proof of (T2) can be sketched out in this way: Substitution in (A2) has the consequence that $(O(p \supset q) \, \& \, Op) \supset O((p \supset q) \, \& \, p)$; since that $(p \supset q) \, \& \, p$ and that $p \, \& \, q$ are equivalent, replacement allows us to say that $(O(p \supset q) \, \& \, Op) \supset O(p \, \& \, q)$; but (A1) tells us that $O(p \, \& \, q) \supset (Op \, \& \, Oq)$, and an axiom derived from propositional calculus has it that $(Op \, \& \, Oq) \supset Oq$; then by transitivity we obtain the result that $(O(p \supset q) \, \& \, Op) \supset Oq$. It should be noted that (T2) justifies the rule of deontic detachment according to which we may deduce the conclusion that Oq from the premises that $O(p \supset q)$ and Op.

A powerful tool is encapsulated in this derived rule of inference: If it is provable in propositional calculus that $p \supset q$, then it is provable in *SDL* that $Op \supset Oq$. The justification for this rule goes as follows: if it is provable in propositional calculus that $p \supset q$, then the propositions that p and that $p \, \& \, q$ are provably equivalent; by replacement in (A1) we get the result that $Op \supset (Op \, \& \, Oq)$, and an axiom tells us that $(Op \, \& \, Oq) \supset Oq$; hence by transitivity we may conclude that it is provable that $Op \supset Oq$. This rule aids us in proving, among others, the following theorems:

(T3) $O \, ((p \vee q) \supset r) \supset O \, (p \supset r) \, \& \, O \, (q \supset r)$
(T4) $O \, (p \supset q) \supset O \, ((p \, \& \, r) \supset q).$

The proofs are obvious once we note that both (T3) and (T4), minus the O-operators, are tautologies of propositional calculus and, thus, provable because it is complete. There are, of course, many other theorems in *SDL*, but those we have explicitly noted can serve as the basis for our subsequent discussion.

Can *SDL* be founded on a theological conception of what ought to be? In order to answer this question we need to provide truth conditions for the formulas of *SDL*. A way of doing this which will turn out to mesh nicely with what we shall be doing in the discussion of other deontic logics makes use of a possible worlds approach to semantics. We think of a possible world as a maximally consistent set of propositions each of which is itself possible. A world which has the proposition that p as a member is a p-world; a p-world is, then, a world in which the proposition that p is true. Tautologies and other necessary truths are true in every possible world; contradictions and other impossibilities are true in none. We assume that the set of all possible worlds is weakly ordered by a relation picked out by the expression 'w_1 is at least as good as w_2'. A weak ordering is one which is both transitive, i.e. for all w_1, w_2 and w_3, if w_1Rw_2 and w_2Rw_3 then w_1Rw_3, and strongly connected, i.e. for all w_1 and w_2, either w_1Rw_2 or w_2Rw_1. We can then define the relation designated by the expression 'w_1 is a better world than w_2' in this way: w_1 is a better world than w_2 if and only if it is not the case that w_2 is at least as good as w_1. Our definitions allow for ties in the sense that two worlds may be equally good, and they allow for the possibility that for any world there is a better. Given these assumptions, we may then stipulate the following definition:

(D1) Op = Def Some p-world is a better world than any ∼p-world.

The intuitive idea is that something ought to be just in case it is in the best worlds or, if none are best, in all sufficiently good worlds. This truth condition is adequate to the system *SDL* in the sense that all the axioms of *SDL* are truths and the inference rules preserve truth no matter how the worlds are ordered by our relation. Hence, all the theorems of *SDL* will be valid formulas under this definition. This should be obvious after a bit of reflection, but perhaps it is worth presenting the outline of an argument for it in order to make things as clear as crystal. First, the axioms derived from tautologies of propositional calculus are valid because they are substitution instances of tautologies. If some p&q-world is better than any ∼(p&q)-world, then some p-world is better than any ∼p-world and some q-world is better than any ∼q-world; hence, (A1) is valid. If some p-world is better than any ∼p-world and some q-world is better than any $\sim$q-world, then some p&q-world is better than any $\sim$(p&q)-world; thus, (A2) is valid. Since there are no f-worlds, it is always the case that $\sim$Of; therefore, (A3) is valid. So all the axioms are valid. Second, consider the rules of inference. The rules of *modus ponens* and uniform substitution preserve validity. Because tautologically equivalent formulas are true at exactly the same worlds, replacement of one by another preserves validity. Moreover, if it is provable that p $\supset$ q, then the set of p-worlds is a subset of the set of q-worlds, and so, if some p-world is better than any $\sim$p-world, then some q-world is better than any $\sim$q-world; hence, our derived rule preserves validity. So all the rules of inference preserve validity. Therefore, all the theorems of *SDL* are valid formulas, given (D1).

Providing foundations for this semantics in theological terms is then an easy task. We may think of divine commands as being either fulfilled (obeyed) or violated (disobeyed). Using this notion, we may say that w_1 is a better world than w_2 just in case w_1 is such that more divine commands are fulfilled in it than are fulfilled in w_2. This allows us to replace (D1) with the following definition:

(D2) Op = Def Some p-world is such that more divine commands
           are fulfilled in it than are fulfilled in any $\sim$p-world.

Here the intuitive idea is that one possible world is better than another provided that in the first more divine commands are fulfilled (obeyed) than in the second. Then something ought to be exactly if some world in which it is the case is a world where more divine commands are fulfilled (obeyed) than any world in which it is not the case. For the sake of simplicity I am supposing that the divine commands in question are those promulgated in the actual world; as long as we do not have to consider iterated occurrences of the O-operator this will suffice. One other point is worth noticing. According to (D2), if there are no divine commands, either because there is no God or because God issues no decrees, then there is no proposition such that it ought to be the case because no world is better than any other. Without divine commands, nothing is obligatory and, if we define the permitted in the usual way, everything is permitted. This is a result we have run across before in other chapters.

In the light of the adequacy of (D1), we can claim that (D2) establishes that *SDL* can be given a theological foundation. Weak orderings of possible worlds in terms of the extent to which the divine commands of the actual world are fulfilled yields *SDL* as a suitable logic of what ought to be. Thus *SDL* is compatible with a divine command conception of what ought to be.

2

It is no secret that philosophical critics have been less than satisfied with *SDL*. One of the main problems centres on finding a way to represent propositions about conditional obligation or, more generally, what ought to be given certain circumstances, using the grammatical resources of *SDL*. Consider, for instance, the claim that, given that Nelson Rockefeller is rich, it ought to be that he gives to the United Fund. Within systems like *SDL* it seems that there are two candidates for a formula to represent such conditional ought-statements. One might take the conditional to be expressed by something to the effect that $O(R \supset G)$, or one might represent it by the claim that $R \supset O(G)$ provided the rules of *SDL* were relaxed to admit such mixed expressions as well-formed. But either way quickly leads to difficulties, as we can see by looking at a celebrated example.

Suppose Jones is wondering whether to go to the assistance of his neighbours. It could well be that each of the following statements is true in such a situation:

(I) It ought to be that Jones goes to the assistance of his neighbours.

(II) It ought to be that if Jones goes to the assistance of his neighbours he tells them he is coming.

(III) If Jones does not go to the assistance of his neighbours, then it ought to be that he does not tell them he is coming.

(IV) Jones does not go to the assistance of his neighbours.

The problem arises when we try to formalize these statements using the grammatical resources of *SDL*, enlarged to allow mixed formulas. The most natural formulation would seem to be the following:

(1) $O(A)$
(2) $O(A \supset T)$
(3) $\sim A \supset O(\sim T)$
(4) $\sim A$.

But from (1) and (2), using the rule of deontic detachment justified by (T2), we may infer that $O(T)$, and from (3) and (4), using the ordinary rule of detachment, we may infer that $O(\sim T)$. The conjunction of these two conclusions, $O(T)$ & $O(\sim T)$, is, however, inconsistent with (T1). The point, it should be emphasized, is not that *SDL* is inconsistent; rather, it is that *SDL* is inconsistent with a certain number of intuitively plausible claims represented in a certain way. Noticing the lack of similarity between (2) and (3), one might think to restore symmetry to the situation by revising the representation either by replacing (2) with (2'): $A \supset O(T)$, or by replacing (3) with (3'): $O(\sim A \supset \sim T)$. In the first case, the use of the deontic detachment rule would be blocked, and in the second the use of the ordinary detachment rule would be blocked. In neither case could we infer that $O(T)$ & $O(\sim T)$. The trouble with this proposal is that both revisions can be seen to lead to misrepresentations of the original statements. On the one hand, since $\sim A \supset (\sim A \lor O(T))$, (4) has (2') as a consequence, though (IV) does not imply (II). On the other, since $O(A) \supset O(A \lor \sim T)$ and $O(A \lor \sim T) \supset O(\sim A \supset \sim T)$, (3') is a consequence of (1), though (I) does not imply (III). Either symmetrization procedure blocks the threatening inference at the price of misrepresenting at least one of its original premisses. This result may be called 'the puzzle of the contrary-to-duty imperative' or, after its creator, 'Chisholm's Puzzle'.[3]

In addition to the problem Chisholm's Puzzle raises for *SDL*, several of its theorems have been thought to be counter-intuitive. Let us focus on two examples. First consider (T3). Suppose that Smith snatches a shipwrecked sailor from the stormy sea. It seems plausible to say that, confronted with the sailor's apparently lifeless body, it ought to be that, if the

---

[3] The puzzle was first set out in R. M. Chisholm, 'Contrary-to-Duty Imperatives and Deontic Logic', *Analysis* 23 (1963), pp. 33–6.

sailor is unconscious or dead, then Smith gives him artificial respiration. But it does not appear at all plausible to say that it both ought to be that if the sailor is unconscious then Smith gives him artificial respiration and ought to be that if the sailor is dead then Smith gives him artificial respiration.[4] If what seems intuitively correct on this score is in fact correct, then the case provides a counter-example to (T3); at least it does so if we take (T3) to represent adequately conditionals of the sort in the example. Think next about (T4). Suppose Brown is employed by DuPont. It seems plausible to say that it ought to be that if Brown is employed by DuPont then DuPont pays Brown's wages. Yet it is implausible to assert that it ought to be that if Brown is employed by DuPont and does no work at all owing to sheer laziness, then DuPont pays Brown's wages. Again, if what seems plausible is actually correct, then (T4) does not express a truth either, at least not a truth about conditional obligations.[5] Surely additional circumstances do sometimes modify, override, or cancel obligations. Finally, even (T1) can be called into question. As we observed in an earlier chapter, some philosophers have had the temerity to challenge it. Suppose Jean-Paul is considering whether to care for his aged mother or to join the maquis, and he cannot do both. Then, according to the objection, it ought to be that he cares for his mother and it ought to be that he does not care for his mother, which is, if true, a counter-example to (T1).[6]

If we acknowledge that some or all of these problems constitute genuine difficulties for *SDL*, then we must next ask how *SDL* can be revised, either by weakening or by supplementation, to generate solutions to the problems whose force we will admit. I shall consider three such revisionary proposals in the following sections. The discussion will be mainly organized around the ways in which the several revised truth conditions for ought-statements allow us to cope with Chisholm's Puzzle.

3

Because he believes that (T1) is a substantive ethical claim rather than a part of the logic of ethical discourse, van

---

[4] This case is considered in Hansson, op. cit., p. 392.

[5] A similar example is discussed in Hansson, op. cit., p. 393.

[6] This issue is treated in some detail in Bas C. van Fraassen, 'Values and the Heart's Command', *The Journal of Philosophy* 70 (1973), pp. 5–19.

Fraassen proposes a weakened truth condition, one of whose consequences will be that (T1) is no longer a valid formula. We are to think of imperatives as divided into those which are in force and those which are not. When an imperative is in force, we ask whether it is fulfilled or violated in various possible worlds. Hence, for each imperative I, there is a set of possible worlds W (I) in which I is fulfilled. The truth definition which van Fraassen proposes may then be stated in the following way:

(D3) Op = Def Some imperative I which is in force is such that W (I) is a subset of the set of all p-worlds.[7]

Intuitively speaking, the definition says that it ought to be that p just in case, for some I which is in force, every possible situation in which I is fulfilled is one in which the proposition that p is true. Let us also assume, along with van Fraassen, that any single imperative, taken by itself, is possible to fulfil. What modifications in our logic are brought about by replacing (D1) with (D3) plus the subsidiary assumption just stated?

In the first place, (T1) is no longer a valid formula. Under (D3) it can happen that, for some p, some imperative in force I is such that W (I) is a subset of the set of p-worlds and some other imperative I* is such that W(I*) is a subset of the set of ∼p-worlds. In this case, we have the result that Op & O∼p, which is inconsistent with (T1). So van Fraassen's truth condition achieves its primary aim, namely, eliminating (T1) from the stock of valid formulas.

But there are other consequences of the revision in our truth condition which are worth mentioning. Since the set of f-worlds is the empty set, which is itself its only subset, there is no imperative I in force such that W(I) is a subset of the set of f-worlds, provided only every imperative is possible to fulfil, that is, is such that W(I) is not the empty set. Hence, given our subsidiary assumption, (A3) remains a valid formula under (D3). Moreover, our derived rule of inference still preserves validity. If the set of p-worlds is a subset of the set of q-worlds and if some imperative in force I is such that W (I) is a subset of the set of p-worlds, then some imperative in force, namely I itself, is such that W(I) is a subset of the set of q-worlds.

---

[7] See van Fraassen, 'Values and the Heart's Command', p. 16.

Hence, if it is provable in propositional calculus that p ⊃q, then the formula which says that Op ⊃Oq is valid under the condition expressed by (D3). Therefore, theorems of *SDL* such as (A1), (T3), and (T4) which can be proved using only this derived rule plus tautologies and rules of propositional calculus remain valid under our new truth condition. However, (A2) is no longer a valid formula. Some p and q may be such that there is an imperative in force I such that W(I) is a subset of the set of p& ∼q-worlds and there is some imperative in force I* such that W(I*) is a subset of the set of q& ∼p-worlds, and yet there is no imperative in force I** such that W(I**) is a subset of the set of p&q-worlds. This would be the case, for example, if I and I* were the only imperatives in force. In such a case, the antecedent of (A2) would be true but its consequent would be false, and this suffices to show that (A2) is not a valid formula under the revised truth definition. In addition, (T2) is no longer a valid formula. Some p and q may be such that there is some I in force such that W(I) is a subset of the set of ∼p& ∼q-worlds, in which case it is true that O(∼p) and, hence, that O(∼p v q) or that O(p ⊃q), and there is some I* in force such that W(I*) is a subset of the set of p & ∼q-worlds, in which case it is true that Op, and yet there is no I** in force such that W(I**) is a subset of the set of q-worlds, in which case it is not true that Oq. We might, of course, have suspected that (T1) and (T2) would not remain valid formulas under the new definition had we recalled that the proofs of both in *SDL* made use of (A2), which is itself no longer valid once we have adopted (D3).

In brief, our new deontic logic is similar to *SDL* in that it includes among its valid formulas (A1), (A3), (T3) and (T4) but differs from *SDL* because (A2), (T1) and (T2) are no longer valid formulas. The revision of (D3) which will set the new logic up on theological foundations is obvious. We need only replace (D3) with this minimally modified definition:

(D4) Op = Def For some divine command C which is in force W(C) is a subset of the set of p-worlds.

The intuition here is that the proposition that p ought to be the case exactly when some divine command in force is such that every possible world where it is fulfilled is also a world where the proposition that p is the case. As a consequence, if there are no divine commands, either because there is no God or because God gives no orders, then there is nothing which ought to be. Without God, nothing is obligatory and everything is permitted.

How does this logical system fare when confronted with the problems which plagued *SDL*? Since (T3) and (T4) are valid formulas under the truth condition expressed by (D3) or (D4), objections to them can be directed with as much plausibility against the revised logic as against *SDL*. But since (T1) is no longer a valid formula, one of the objections to *SDL* is met. Moreover, the truth condition expressed by (D3) or (D4) provides us with a solution to Chisholm's Puzzle. In the first place, since (T2) is no longer a valid formula, the rule of deontic detachment no longer preserves validity, and so we may cease to regard the inference from (1) and (2) to the conclusion that O(T) as unproblematic. More important, even if that conclusion can be gotten from the particular premisses of Chisholm's Puzzle, the conclusion that O(T) & O($\sim$T) is no longer inconsistent with a valid formula of our deontic logic once (T1) is no longer valid.

In terms of the problems we suggested constitute objections of some gravity to *SDL*, it is clear that the revision van Fraassen proposes is an improvement over *SDL* because it solves some of them. But others remain, as does the suspicion that, using only the material conditional and the O-operator, we do not have a way to express adequately statements of conditional obligation and other conditional ought-statements. This suggests that another method of trying to deal with our problems would involve enriching *SDL* by adding to it a new primitive dyadic operator or sentential connective, symbolized by 'O(q/p)', intended to express 'q is obligatory in the circumstances that p' or 'It ought to be that q, given that p.' We may ask how truth conditions are to be provided for this locution.

4

There are in the recent literature several logical systems intended by their creators to give an account of the logic of conditional obligation or of circumstantial ought-statements. Underlying most of them is the intuition that, when circumstances rule out the best, what ought to be becomes the best that can be under the circumstances. For our present purposes the clearest and most direct way to capture this idea is in terms of the following definition:

(D5) $O(q/p)$ = Def Some q&p-world is better than any ~q&p-world.

The truth condition expressed by (D5) is related in simple ways to others found in the technical literature. It is a special case of one of the conditions discussed by Lewis because his condition makes provision for the ordering of possible worlds to vary with the world chosen as the point of reference, as (D5) does not.[8] According to this conception, different preference orderings among worlds may obtain from the points of view of different worlds; speaking theologically, it is as if God commands different things in different possible worlds. The condition expressed by (D5) is also a special case of a condition considered by van Fraassen which allows, as (D5) does not, that several values may be realized at each world with some worlds having no greatest value there realized.[9] On the other hand, (D5) differs from the truth condition in each of the three systems discussed by Hansson, the last of which is also considered by Lewis.[10] Since no possible world contains a contradiction, it is never the case that some q&f-world is better than any ~q&f-world. Hence, it is never the case that $O(q/f)$; nothing is obligatory in contradictory circumstances or impossible conditions. But in Hansson's systems everything turns out to be obligatory under impossible conditions.

It would, I think, be silly to suppose that our intuitions about impossible circumstances would be a reliable guide to choosing between alternative conceptions of conditional obligation on the basis of this difference. It is, however, worth noting that, given (D5), if we assume with some theists that the non-existence of God is an impossible circumstance, we can retrieve the familiar conclusion that nothing is obligatory in conditions where God does not exist.

[8] David Lewis, *Counterfactuals*, Oxford: Basil Blackwell (1973), pp. 100–4.
[9] Bas C. van Fraassen, 'The Logic of Conditional Obligation', *Journal of Philosophical Logic* 1 (1972), pp. 417–38.
[10] See Hansson, op. cit., p. 397 and Lewis, op. cit., p. 103.

The several generalizations of and alternatives to (D5) are not without technical interest, but from (D5) without additional complications we can get some understanding of the logic of conditional obligation and circumstantial ought-statements. Consider first the analogue of the problematic (T3), which can be written as follows:

$$O(r/p \vee q) \supset O(r/p) \ \& \ O(r/q).$$

It is not difficult to show that this formula is not valid under definition (D5). Suppose that w_1, the best world, is an $r \& p \& \sim q$-world, that w_2, the next best world, is a $\sim r \& p \& \sim q$-world, and that w_3, the third best world, is a $\sim r \& \sim p \& q$-world. Then some $r \& (p \vee q)$-world, namely w_1, is better than any $\sim r \& (p \vee q)$-world, and so $O(r/p \vee q)$. But some $\sim r \& q$-world, namely w_3, is better than any $r \& q$-world, and so $\sim O(r/q)$. Hence there is a counter-example to the formula in question for some ordering of possible worlds, and so it is not valid under (D5). This suffices to solve one of the problems which plagued the representation of conditional obligation in terms of material implication in *SDL*.

Consider next the analogue of (T4) which can be written in the following way:

$$O(q/p) \supset O(q/p \& r).$$

Suppose that the best world, w_1, is a $p \& q \& \sim r$-world, that the next best world, w_2, is a $p \& \sim q \& r$-world, and that the third best world, w_3, is a $p \& q \& r$-world. Some $q \& p$-world, namely w_1, is better than any $\sim q \& p$-world, and so $O(q/p)$. But, some $\sim q \& p \& r$-world, namely w_2, is better than any $q \& p \& r$-world, and so $\sim O(q/p \& r)$. Therefore, this formula is not valid under (D5) either. Moreover, as we should expect, the following formula is not valid:

$$O(q/p \& r) \supset O(q/p).$$

For suppose that the best world, w_1, is a $p \& \sim q \& \sim r$-world, that the next best world, w_2, is a $p \& q \& r$-world, and that the third best world, w_3, is a $p \& \sim q \& r$-world. On this assumption, some $q \& p \& r$-world, namely w_2, is better than any $\sim q \& p \& r$-world, and so $O(q/p \& r)$. But some $\sim q \& p$-world, namely w_1, is better than any $q \& p$-world, and so $\sim O(q/p)$. This suffices to show that the formula in question is not valid. The combination of the last two results is welcome because it allows that there can be consistent alternating sequences like the following: Given that Robin Hood robs the rich, it ought to be that he returns the money; but given that Robin Hood robs the rich and gives to the poor, it ought to be that he does not return the money; but given that Robin Hood robs the rich and gives to the poor and beggars the rich, it ought to be that he returns the money; and so forth. In short, (D5) allows for the appearance and disappearance of conditional obligations as circumstances alter; this is how the phenomenon of overriding is reflected in the logic of conditional obligation. This is a good thing because it is a standard criticism of some of the older logics of conditional obligation that they do not make such allowances.[11]

We can also use (D5) to solve Chisholm's Puzzle. The appropriate representation of (I)–(IV) in terms of our dyadic operator is this:

(a) $O(A)$
(b) $O(T/A)$
(c) $O(\sim T/\sim A)$
(d) $\sim A$.

Suppose that the best world, w_1, is an A&T-world, that the next best world, w_2, is a $\sim$A&$\sim$T-world, that the third best world, w_3, is an A&$\sim$T-world, and that the fourth best world, w_4, is a $\sim$A&T-world. Since some A-world, namely w_1, is better than any $\sim$A-world, $O(A)$. Thus (a) expresses a truth in this model. Because some T&A-world, namely w_1, is better than any $\sim$T&A-world, $O(T/A)$. Hence (b) also expresses a truth. And since some $\sim$T&$\sim$A-world, namely w_2, is better than any T&$\sim$A-world, $O(\sim T/\sim A)$. Therefore (c) expresses a truth too. To these assumptions we may add the supposition that $\sim A$, which amounts only to the claim that the actual world is neither w_1 nor w_3, though it may, of course, be much worse than even the fourth best world. Therefore, our suppositions provide a model for (a)–(d) and thereby for the premises

---

[11] Hansson directs this criticism against older systems formulated by Rescher and von Wright. See Hansson, op. cit., pp. 393–4.

which generate Chisholm's Puzzle. In addition, since some T-world, namely w_1, is better than any $\sim$T-world, we may conclude that O(T). But it is not the case that some $\sim$T-world is better than any T-world, and so we may also say that $\sim$O($\sim$T). These conclusions, far from being inconsistent with what (T1) of *SDL* asserts, provide a true instance of (T1). Therefore, once we have represented (II) and (III) of Chisholm's Puzzle in terms of the dyadic operator of conditional obligation as (b) and (c), the puzzle is easily solved.

We may conclude, then, that (D5) allows us to resolve our worries about conditional obligations and circumstantial ought-statements. However, it does not solve the problem about incompatible unconditional obligations. This is easy to appreciate when we grasp the fact that the unconditional ought-operator of *SDL* can be defined in terms of our conditional ought-operator. Let 't' stand for an arbitrarily selected tautology of propositional calculus. According to (D5), O(p/t) if and only if some p&t-world is better than any $\sim$p&t-world. Because it is necessary that t, t is a member of every possible world. Hence, the p&t-worlds are just the p-worlds, and the $\sim$p&t-worlds are just the $\sim$p-worlds. Thus, some p&t-world is better than any $\sim$p&t-world exactly if some p-world is better than any $\sim$p-world. And, according to (D1), this is so just in case Op. Therefore, Op $\equiv$ O(p/t). What ought to be unconditionally is what ought to be given tautologous conditions. Since (D1) specifies a condition under which (T1) is a valid formula, the more general definition expressed by (D5) does not allow conflicting unconditional obligations. So, if this issue created problems for *SDL*, they are not solved by the logic associated with (D5). Still, since that logic has solutions to the other problems which confronted *SDL*, it is an improvement over *SDL*.

It is also quite simple to bring this logic into line with our theological preoccupations. What needs to be done is to restate (D5) in terms of divine commands. Relying on the idea that one possible world is better than another just when the first is such that more divine commands are fulfilled in it than are fulfilled in the second, we may formulate the theological replacement for (D5) in this way:

(D6) O(q/p) = Def Some q&p-world is such that more divine
commands are fulfilled in it than in any
~q&p-world.

By inspection of (D6) we learn that if there are no divine commands, either because there is no God or because God never
gives commands, then no world fulfils any divine commands
and, thus, no world fulfils more than any other. In such a case,
it would never be that O(q/p), no matter what propositions
'p' and 'q' stand for. Without divine commands, nothing
ought to be no matter what the circumstances. Therefore, the
moral libertinism, so to speak, of some divine command
theories in the absence of divine commands is carried along
into the theological foundations of the logic of conditional
obligation.

5

Since *SDL* can be extended by way of (D5) or (D6) to
encompass conditional obligation or circumstantial ought-
statements, we might next wonder whether the weaker logic
whose truth condition is given by (D3) or (D4) can also be
modified to include such conditionals. An affirmative answer is
provided by the following definition, proposed by van Fraassen:

(D7) O(q/p) = Def Some imperative I in force, which is itself
conditional upon p, is such that the inter-
section of W(I) with the set of p-worlds is a
subset of the set of q-worlds.[12]

What does it mean to say that an imperative is conditional
upon something? Van Fraassen assumes that such an imperative
can be fulfilled or violated only if its condition is the case.[13]
On this assumption, if some imperative I is conditional upon p,
then W(I) is a subset of the set of p-worlds. Using this fact,
we can show that the analogues of (T3) and (T4) are not valid
formulas under the condition specified by (D7). First, suppose
that O(r/pvq). Then there is some imperative I in force, which
is conditional upon pvq, such that the intersection of W(I)
with the set of pvq-worlds is a subset of the set of r-worlds.
Since I is conditional upon pvq, W(I) is a subset of the set of

---

[12] See van Fraassen, 'Values and the Heart's Command', p. 17.
[13] Ibid., p. 16.

pvq-worlds. But it may be that some worlds in W(I) are p& ~q-worlds and others are ~p&q-worlds, and, if so, W(I) is not a subset of the set of p-worlds and is not a subset of the set of q-worlds. Moreover, it may be that I is the only imperative in force. On these suppositions, there is no imperative in force conditional upon p alone and there is no imperative in force conditional upon q alone, and so it is not the case that O(r/p) and it is not the case that O(r/q). Hence, the analogue of (T3) is not a valid formula under (D7). Second, suppose that O(q/p). Then there is some imperative I in force, conditional upon p, such that the intersection of W(I) with the set of p-worlds is a subset of the set of q-worlds. Because I is conditional upon p, W(I) is a subset of the set of p-worlds. But it may be that some worlds in W(I) are p& ~r-worlds, in which case W(I) is not a subset of the set of p&r-worlds. And I may be the only imperative in force. On these suppositions, there is no imperative in force conditional upon p&r, and so it is not the case that O(q/p&r). Hence, the analogue of (T4) is not a valid formula either under (D7). Thus we may say that (D7) solves the problems which (D3) left outstanding.

Theological foundations of the sort appropriate to this conception of conditional obligation can be provided by substituting for (D7), in a manner quite parallel to the way (D4) replaces (D3), the following definition:

(D8) O(q/p) = Def Some divine command C in force, which is itself conditional upon p, is such that the intersection of W(C) with the set of p-worlds is a subset of the set of q-worlds.

This definition has the expected consequence that if there are no divine commands, then, since none are in force, there is nothing obligatory no matter what the circumstances are.

There are, it goes without saying, other approaches to deontic logic and the problems of conditional obligation. One might, for instance, try to base deontic logic upon temporal logic. Along these lines it has been suggested that a simple and plausible solution to Chisholm's Puzzle consists in saying that so long as it is not yet unalterable that Jones does not go to the assistance of his neighbours it ought to be that he both goes to their assistance and tells them he is coming, but once it has become unalterable that he does not go it ought only to be that he does not tell them he is coming.[14] It is certainly not my intention to suggest by omission that I have discussed all the approaches to deontic logic which may prove to be philosophically fruitful.

We can, however, learn one lesson without prolonging the discussion, and it is the only important lesson in the present context. Each of the deontic logics we have been studying can be built on a foundation of divine commands if we provide the appropriate truth condition, though each can as well be erected on other foundations. Thus we may allow philosophical considerations of a non-theological sort to guide our preferences among systems of deontic logic without fear that the resulting preferences will yield a logic inconsistent with a divine command conception of ethics. This is as things should be according to the notion that logic is and ought to be neutral among competing substantive ethical claims and moral theories. Surely we would not wish the logic of the concept of obligation or, more broadly, the logic of ought-statements, to settle the question either for or against divine command theories. All the approaches to deontic logic we have examined are, as they should be, neutral in the dispute between theological and non-theological ethical theories. This is reassuring but also a bit disappointing. Since systems of deontic logic can be based either on theological foundations or on any one of a number of alternative substructures inconsistent with divine command theories, deontic logic will never be of the slightest help either in attacking or in defending divine command theories so long as deontic logic preserves its proper neutrality. In this sense deontic logic is irrelevant to the effort to prove or to refute divine command theories. And it is equally irrelevant to the endeavour of defending such theories against objections.

---

[14] A recent discussion of this approach is found in P. S. Greenspan, 'Conditional Oughts and Hypothetical Imperatives', *The Journal of Philosophy* 72 (1975), pp. 259–76.

VI

Divine Justice and Divine Mercy

It is often alleged that divine command theories of ethics are theologically unacceptable because they do not permit a coherent account of the moral attributes of God to be formulated. If we adopt one of the stronger divine command theories and suppose that only divine commands impose moral requirements on us, then obedience to God is a fundamental human virtue. We may take the virtue of obedience to God to be a settled habit which a person has just in case he is disposed to do whatever God commands. If we also assume that the exercise of a moral virtue consists in obedience to a moral law because one believes that one is acting as morality requires, then obedience to God is the most basic moral virtue. Other moral virtues will then be such that exercising them will entail being obedient to God. Thus, for example, temperance will be the disposition to obey those divine commands which require us to refrain from excesses of certain sorts. And courage will be the disposition to obey those divine commands which require us to act bravely in certain hazardous situations.

But, within this framework, the divine command theorist does not seem to be able to speak coherently of God having moral virtues. For it is very odd, and perhaps unintelligible, to suppose that God, or anyone else for that matter, commands himself to do certain things and then obeys the commands he has addressed to himself. If a certain man is captain of a ship, then the crew is under his command, and he may command them and they must obey him. But he does not command himself. The admiral of the fleet addresses commands to him, and he must obey the admiral's commands. No one, then, is in a position to issue commands to God or to exact obedience from him. We may, I suppose, if we care to think about God in crudely anthropomorphic terms, imagine God saying to himself on a certain occasion, 'You really must now come to the aid of your Chosen People; they have suffered long enough!' Or, we may imagine the mental life of God to be such that he runs through little pieces of practical reasoning when he deliberates about what he will do. Despite their crudity, these imaginative pictures show how we might think of God telling himself what to do. But such pictures do not, I think, represent God as commanding himself to do certain things; they represent him as in the process of deciding what he will do. If God goes ahead and does what he tells himself to do, then he is not obeying a command which he has addressed to himself; instead he is simply doing what he has decided to do. And, if God does something other than what he tells himself to do, he is not disobeying a command he has addressed to himself; rather he has changed his mind and is only, after all, doing what he has finally chosen to do. Since no one, not even God, could be correctly said to obey or to disobey an imperative which did not originate from a source apart from himself, it is not possible for God, or for anyone else, to address commands to himself. But then, given our assumptions, since God cannot have the virtue of being obedient to God, he cannot possess any of the other human moral virtues.

God can, of course, love us and treat us with kindness, and perhaps he is such that necessarily he loves us and treats us with kindness. But nothing does, or could, require him to do these things, and so he is obedient to no command or moral law in so doing. If God does love us and treat us with kindness, he does not exercise moral virtues when he acts in these ways. God simply does what he chooses to do, or what his nature constrains him to do; whatever he does, he satisfies no moral requirements and exhibits no moral virtues. We might say that God cannot be dutiful because he is not subject to a moral law not of his own making. He cannot either do or fail to do his duty since he has no duties in the sense in which we have duties.[1] But, if God cannot have moral virtues, then it would

---

[1] Robert M. Adams, 'A Modified Divine Command Theory of Ethical Wrong-

seem that he cannot have those moral excellences which are logically necessary conditions for being worthy of worship. Surely, though, it is a criterion of adequacy for an account of God's nature which pretends to give a satisfactory description of the beliefs of orthodox theists that God is worthy of the sorts of worship practised in the major theistic religions.

Hence, our first task must be to work out in some detail a doctrine about the nature of God which allows us to attribute to him some excellences of character which are, according to divine command theories, the analogues of moral virtues that we ought to possess.

I

In order not to make our task too simple, let us work with a version of divine command theory according to which divine commands and moral requirements are coextensive, and necessarily so. Let the letter 'x' be a variable, ranging over persons; thus, substituends for 'x' will be terms such as names and definite descriptions which designate persons. Let the letter 'A' be a variable ranging over particular actions; hence, substituends for 'A' will be phrases which designate such things as John Brown's raiding Harpers Ferry. We may then adopt the following definition schema:

(D1)   x is obedient to God in doing A = Df x and A are such that God commands that he does it and his belief that God commands that he does it is his reason for doing it.

The second conjunct of the *definiens* is to be understood in such a way that a proposition expressed by a sentence of the form 'x's belief that God commands that x does A is x's reason for doing A' entails both a proposition expressed by a sentence of the form 'x believes that God commands that x does A' and a proposition expressed by a sentence of the form 'x does A'. Also, the occurrences of the variables 'x' and 'A' in the *definiens* are to be taken transparently so that coextensive terms may be substituted for one another without changes in truth-value. Hence, we may say that a certain person is obedient to

---

ness' in *Religion and Morality* (ed. G. Outka and J. P. Reeder), Garden City: Doubleday (1973). This point is made explicitly on p. 339.

God in doing a certain thing just in case God commands him to do that thing, he believes that God commands him to do that thing, he does that thing and his reason for doing it is his belief that God has commanded him to do it.

An interesting philosophical puzzle can be solved with the help of (D1). God could, we may suppose, command that a certain man practises charity for its own sake. How can such a man be obedient to God in a particular act of practising charity? It seems that he confronts a dilemma. On the one hand, if he practises charity in order to fulfil a divine command, he does not practise charity for its own sake and, hence, is not obedient to God in practising charity. On the other hand, if he practises charity but does not do so in order to fulfil a divine command, then his reason for practising charity is something other than a belief that it has been divinely commanded, and, again, he is not obedient to God in practising charity. In either case, it seems that he is not obedient to God in what he does.

The key to solving this puzzle lies, I believe, in recognizing that God has, by hypothesis, commanded not charitable behaviour but rather charitable behaviour for its own sake. What he has commanded is action in a comprehensive sense which includes both outward behaviour and inward motivation. In these circumstances, if the man's belief that God commands that he practises charity for its own sake is his reason for practising charity for its own sake, then he is obedient to God in practising charity for its own sake. The man should not practise charity in order to fulfil a divine command; he has been commanded to practise charity for its own sake. But he should practise charity for its own sake in order to fulfil a divine command, for that is what he has been commanded to do. The horns of the apparent dilemma can be avoided. If the man practises charity for its own sake and does so because he believes that God has commanded that he practises charity for its own sake, then his reason for practising charity for its own sake is his belief that practising charity for its own sake has been divinely commanded, and he is obedient to God in practising charity for its own sake.

Now let the letter 'M' be a variable which ranges over character traits so that substituends for 'M' will be nouns such as 'justice', 'courage', 'fortitude', and 'piety', which designate character traits. Our next definition schema has this form:

(D2)   x exercises the moral virtue of M in doing A = Df A manifests
        M and x is obedient to God in doing A.

To say that a certain action manifests a certain character trait
is to claim that the character trait in question is a disposition
which is a part of the cause of the action in question. Thus, if a
man rescues a drowning child at the risk of his own life, his
action manifests courage just in case his courageous disposition
is part of the cause of the rescue. It is an immediate consequence of (D2) that every moral virtue is such that, if anyone
exercises it in doing any thing, then that person is obedient to
God in doing that thing. In short, any exercise of a moral
virtue entails an act of obedience to God. This is as things
should be within the framework of divine command theories.
According to such theories, to exercise a moral virtue is, among
other things, to do what morality requires, and to do what
morality requires is to obey a divine command.

It would not, I think, be possible to define possession of a
moral virtue in terms of its exercise. Since a moral virtue is a
disposition of a certain sort, someone could possess a moral
virtue without ever exercising it, provided he never happens to
be in circumstances where its exercise would be called for and
feasible. Thus, there may be courageous people who, given the
protected conditions of life in modern industrial societies, never
have the opportunity to display their courage. But we may, I
believe, affirm the following very weak principle about the
connection between possessing a moral virtue and exercising
it:

(P1)   For all persons x and for all character traits M, if x has the
        moral virtue of M, then x and M are such that it is logically
        possible that, for some action A, he exercises it in doing A.

And now it is easy to see why God cannot have any moral
virtues. God is such that it is not possible that, for some action
A, God commands that he does A. Hence, by (D1), God is
such that it is not possible that, for some A, he is obedient to
God in doing A. Then, by (D2), God is such that, for all M,
it is not possible that, for some A, he exercises it in doing A.
And so, by (P1), God is such that, for all M, he does not have

the moral virtue of M. In brief, because God could not be subject to moral requirements generated by his own commands, he could not have moral virtues whose exercise entails obedience to his commands. God, and he alone, is, according to divine command theories, outside the domain of persons to whom it makes sense to attribute moral virtues. Therefore, according to such theories, God does not have, strictly speaking, any moral virtues.

But, of course, God may very well have character traits which are very much like some of the human moral virtues. Even a divine command theorist can claim that God is loving and forgiving. Divine love and human love are, to be sure, different things in the view of a divine command theorist. Human love of the appropriate sort has such properties as being commanded by God and being a moral virtue, but divine love lacks these properties. Since divine love and human love are in this manner discernible, they cannot be identical if we take seriously the principle that if things are identical then whatever is true of one is true of the other. Nevertheless, divine love and human love need not be conceived of as so utterly unlike one another that it is only by equivocation that we use the term 'love' to refer to both. Exercises of divine love and of human love of the appropriate sort may have enough in common, for instance, such features as unselfish concern for the welfare of the recipient, that it makes perfectly good sense to speak of both as varieties of loving. The crucial difference between these two varieties of love is that divine love is not a moral virtue because no requirement for it is imposed on God by divine command while human love is a moral virtue because the requirement that we love one another has been imposed by divine fiat. And so, we may, if we wish, call those excellences of character which are the divine analogues of some of the character traits which even divine command theorists concede to be human moral virtues 'God's virtues'. We are then in a position to ask which virtues are such that God does, or could, possess them.

Obviously, not every human moral virtue could have a divine analogue. If God commands chastity or sexual continence from certain people, then chastity or sexual continence are morally required of such people. In them, chastity or sexual continence are moral virtues. But, since God has no body and, hence, no sexual desires or cravings, chastity and continence are not to be numbered among his virtues. A person without sexual desires could not possess a virtue whose exercise consists in restraining sexual desires when they become unruly, except perhaps in some trivial sense. Or, again, if God has commanded that we be devoted to his worship, then we are morally required to be devout, but even if devoutness is a human moral virtue God does not possess it, for it is inconceivable that God should worship himself. It is only appropriate to worship what one takes to be one's superior in certain respects, and presumably God knows that he has no superior in those respects and that he could not be superior to himself in any respect. It is evident, moreover, that similar remarks would be equally appropriate with reference to such things as divinely ordained dietary laws and divinely ordained religious ceremonials. Even if it is a moral virtue for human beings to be disposed to follow such diets or to take part in such rituals, it could not be a virtue for God to do so.

Other cases are more problematic. It is usually assumed that, in some circumstances at least, we ought to forgive one another offences given and received. We may for the sake of argument suppose that God has commanded certain exercises of forgiveness. If so, such exercises of forgiveness are, for the divine command theorist, morally required, and a forgiving disposition is a human moral virtue. But what does it mean to say that God has a forgiving disposition? And, can God in any sense forgive our sins? As we shall soon see, it is not an easy matter to give reasonable answers to these questions. But answers must be given if the explanatory demands of theistic orthodoxy are to be met.

2

I had suggested in a previous chapter that something is sinful just in case God commands its negation. The sinful is, then, what is contrary to God's commands. For a divine command theorist, the sinful and the morally forbidden are coextensive. We may, therefore, define sinfulness with respect to actions in this way:

(D3) It is sinful that x does A = Df x and A are such that God commands that he does not do it.

This is, it should be noted, a broad definition of the class of sinful actions. A more restrictive definition would include reference to some intentional feature of the agent such as malicious intent. An example of a narrower definition is this:

(D4) It is sinful that x does A = Df x and A are such that God commands that he does not do it and he believes that God commands that he does not do it.

An agent who does something which is sinful in the sense of (D3) but not in the sense of (D4) may be able to excuse himself before God by pleading that he did not mean to do anything contrary to a divine command. Nevertheless, what such an agent does is contrary to God's commands, and so, presumably, it is to some extent offensive to God. God may, for all I know, find it easier to forgive someone who sins without believing that he is sinning than to forgive someone who does what is sinful while believing that what he does is sinful. For our purposes, however, (D3) will suffice to delimit the category of the sinful, for the class of actions defined by (D3) will, if it is not empty, properly include the class of actions defined by (D4) given that there have been people who do not believe that there are any divine commands. If we can give a reasonable account of how it is possible for God to forgive sinful actions as defined by (D3), then we will also have given an account of how God can forgive sinful actions as defined by (D4) or by other narrower definitions.

It is not a simple matter to explain what a divine forgiving disposition might be or to state precisely what God would be doing in exercising such a disposition. All that is clear at the outset is that certain accounts of what it is to forgive sins will not do, especially within the framework of a divine command theory. Sometimes, for example, we speak of one human person forgiving another when what really happens is a reversal of moral judgement in the light of changed beliefs or attitudes. Suppose a father learns in 1970 that his son's college has suspended the son for taking part in a rather turbulent demonstration against the presence of a CIA recruiter on campus. Having a lively sense of patriotism, the father passionately detests what his son has done; believing the CIA to be a guardian of our liberties, the father judges that his son has acted wrongly. He becomes estranged from his son. By 1975, however, the father's passions have cooled, and he has learned that the CIA has been up to some dirty tricks both at home and abroad. He retracts his moral condemnation of the son, and perhaps he even brings himself to approve of his son's action. He tries to repair the breach that has disrupted their relationship for five painful years. We might say about such a case that the father has forgiven his son and that he had good reasons for doing so. It is obvious, however, that God's forgiveness of sins cannot be modelled on the reversal of judgement and attitude represented in this story. In the first place, certain tales from the Old Testament to the contrary notwithstanding, it would be a mistake to think of God as being driven into a frenzy of detestation or uncontrolled passion. God's attitudes, we may suppose, are always appropriate to their objects. In the second place, being omniscient, God has no occasion to give up beliefs in the light of new evidence or to reverse his moral judgements. Indeed, this point is particularly clear in divine command theories. Presumably God would know what he himself has forbidden and, hence, what is sinful, even were he less than omniscient merely in virtue of being ignorant of some recondite mathematical truth. God could not, it seems evident, make a mistaken judgement about what is sinful. If he also knows what every human agent ever does, then he will never have occasion to reverse his moral judgements no matter what people do. For this reason, God cannot forgive our sins in the same way the father can forgive his son's participation in the demonstration.

There are cases of another sort in which a kind of forgiveness which is sometimes virtuous in human interactions could not appropriately be exercised by God. Suppose a man has promised his friend to repay on Friday the shilling he borrowed on Wednesday. When Friday rolls around, he is simply too lazy to walk down the hall to his friend's office to hand over the shilling, but on Monday when they meet in the elevator he pays his debt. The friend might condone this minor act of promise-breaking; he might decide to overlook it, to forget about it or to treat it as if it had never taken place. The friend might in this sense be said to have forgiven an act of promise-breaking, although this is a rather pompous way of putting it because the offence was so slight. However, to condone an offence is not always to exercise a human moral virtue. Someone who condones genocide, who overlooks it, or treats it as if it had never occurred, would exhibit an extreme form of moral insensitivity according to our usual ways of thinking about such matters. If God is omniscient, he cannot literally overlook or forget about actions contrary to his commands; he knows about all such actions. I suppose that God might treat such actions as if they had never occurred in the sense that he could decline to chastise anyone who acted contrary to his commands. But, if he did respond in this way, one could reasonably suspect that he exhibited a certain frivolity in commanding which would be unbecoming in a being worthy of worship. If God declined to regard disobedience to his commands as a serious matter, then the equation of what is commanded by God and what is morally required would seem exceedingly unreasonable. A divine command theorist who acknowledges that moral requirements are serious matters is constrained to admit that divine commands are also matters of consequence, and so he should not claim that God would treat disobedience to his commands as if it had never occurred. Moreover, the view of most orthodox theists is that God regards certain sins as very grave offences, meriting extreme punishment, and yet he is prepared to forgive even such sins. And it would clearly not be reasonable to suppose that, if God forgives the sin of a repentant murderer, he thereby condones a murder.

Yet another kind of case in which it would be appropriate to speak of human forgiveness but inappropriate to speak of divine forgiveness involves violation of a rule when mitigating circumstances are present. Suppose a poor man steals apples from my orchard to feed his starving children. Technically speaking, he is guilty of theft. If we live in a society where people are not very secure in possession of their property, the legally required penalty for thefts of even minor sorts might be rather severe. But a wise judge might decide that our poor man ought not to be found guilty of theft, and I might concur in such a decision, because the poor man's circumstances completely excuse his action. More generally, rules, either legal or moral, may apply correctly to only the majority of cases; special cases may, when properly understood, count as exceptions to such rules. To forgive in such special cases is merely to decide that someone who has violated the letter of the law has not violated its spirit. An omniscient God, however, does not need to promulgate laws to which exceptions might arise. If he lays down laws for us which are over-simplified as a concession to our limited capacity for dealing with complexity, he can use rules as complicated as need be to form his own judgements about guilt and innocence in a fashion which leaves no gap between the letter and the spirit of his laws. God, we suppose, never needs to make exceptions to the rules he uses in order to insure that a case is treated as it deserves to be handled. Moreover, God's forgiveness of sins is supposed to extend even to those actions which are evidently not exceptions to moral rules, and which violate his laws in the absence of mitigating circumstances. Thus, according to orthodox theists, God could forgive even the sins of Eichmann, though from the point of view of human morality some of the things Eichmann did are unforgivable. Within the framework of a divine command theory the difficulty becomes even more pronounced. If we suppose that what is dictated by divine command is co-extensive with what is morally required, and necessarily so, then there could not be exceptions on moral grounds to the requirements imposed by divine commands. If our poor man is not required by morality to refrain from pilfering from my orchard, then God cannot have commanded that he refrain from stealing my fruit. There are moral exceptions to human legal and moral rules only if these exceptions are already built into the structure of God's decrees. Thus, God cannot judge that someone who is technically guilty of acting contrary to one of his commands is actually innocent morally speaking since his commands define what is to count as moral guilt and moral innocence.

After examining cases like the three I have just discussed, plus some others I will consider later on when I treat of God's mercy, Anne C. Minas investigates situations in which forgiveness involves a change of attitude on the part of whoever does the forgiving. She argues that God, as usually thought of by orthodox theists, cannot exercise forgiveness in this sense either.[2]

---

[2] Anne C. Minas, 'God and Forgiveness', *Philosophical Quarterly* 25 (1975), pp. 138–50.

Because I believe that divine forgiveness does indeed involve either a change of attitude on God's part or an act of refraining from adopting a certain negative attitude by God, I propose to analyse this argument at some length and to show that it is unsound.

We may appropriately speak of one human being forgiving another when the forgiving party gives up an attitude of resentment directed toward the party being forgiven. Suppose, by way of illustration, that Jones, while driving carelessly, hits Smith, causing him to be paralysed. Smith resents the injury Jones has done him, and justifiably so, but he may deliberately forswear such resentment, particularly if Jones exhibits remorse or repents of his carelessness. If Smith gives up his resentment by, say, repudiating the bitter feelings he has about Jones and trying to extirpate them, he has forgiven Jones for having caused his paralysis. Minas holds that a person can only resent what he takes to be harm or injury done to him. From this assumption she draws the conclusion that a perfect being could not harbour resentment. Two reasons are set forth in support of this claim. First, 'taking an injury personally, as opposed to having a general sense of its wrongness, is a distinctly human failing, an imperfection'.[3] Second, nothing could harm or injure a perfect being, and so 'his very perfection should make him immune from the kind of injury which makes forgiveness appropriate'.[4] If God is perfect, nothing we can do could harm him. Since he is omniscient, he knows that whatever we may do will not injure him. Hence, he never takes what we do as causing injury to him, and indeed could not do so. Therefore, he never resents what we do because such resentment would be unreasonable and an imperfection. And, since he never harbours resentment, he never is in a position to forswear it. According to Minas, if forgiveness consists in giving up the attitude of resentment, then God never exercises forgiveness because he never has the attitude of resentment.

Let me begin my attack on this argument with a parable. A philosopher-king legislates for his people. Being very wise, he contrives laws which, if obeyed, will insure that the welfare

[3] Ibid., p. 147.   [4] Ibid., p. 149.

of his people will be secured. He does this because he loves his people and is concerned for their welfare. His laws prohibit such things as murder, rape, torture, and the like. Unfortunately, some of the people disobey the laws and injure each other. The philosopher-king is not himself injured or harmed by such acts of disobedience as do occur, but he is offended. Being philosophical by temper and training, he does not brood or sulk when he is thus offended, but he does adopt a negative attitude toward those who disobey the laws he has laid down. He regards the offenders with displeasure and disfavour and is disposed to have them punished. As it happens, some of the offenders repent; they exhibit remorse, form intentions to obey the laws thenceforth, and begin trying to act obediently. The philosopher-king does not forget their offences, but, knowing that they have repudiated their acts of disobedience and are endeavouring to obey the laws, he forswears his negative attitude toward them. He ceases to look on them with displeasure or disfavour and loses the inclination to punish them. They are now, he tells himself, reformed characters. They regret what they once did to detract from the welfare of his people, and they are now trying to do things which contribute to the welfare of his people. And so he decides that it would be pointless for him to nurse a grudge against them.

Perhaps there never has been and never will be a philosopher-king. But the parable seems to be logically coherent. If it is, then Minas is mistaken about several things. In the first place, a lawgiver can be offended at disobedient acts and offended by those who do them without being harmed or injured by such people or their actions. Indeed, one need not be a lawgiver to be offended by actions which, though they do one no harm, are contrary to the law. It may be that I care very little about the roadside scenery and am not injured if it is cluttered with beer cans, and yet I am offended when I see people throwing beer cans out their car windows just because I know that there are people who do care about the roadside scenery and are distressed when it is made to look ugly by litterbugs. In the second place, someone who is offended by the disobedience of another has some negative attitudes or dispositions directed toward the offender. Perhaps it is not easy to name the attitudes in question with precision without making misleading suggestions. For example, the word 'resentment' may suggest such diverse things as feelings of rage, nursing a grudge, and spiteful tendencies. If so, then it is not in every case an appropriate description of the negative attitude the offended party has, and it is never the correct way to describe God's attitude when he is offended. It may be that some more neutral word such as 'displeasure' better describes the attitude theists suppose God has when one of us disobeys him. Finally, someone who has been offended can give up such negative attitudes, and properly so, provided that the offender exhibits remorse and intends to try to avoid acting offensively in the future. Therefore, a person who has been offended but not harmed can exercise forgiveness.

Moreover, as I have described things, there is no reason for thinking that God could not be offended by our sins and could not, subsequently, withdraw the displeasure with which he regards us when we have sinned, provided we repent of having sinned.[5] Within the framework of a divine command theory of ethics, it is especially easy to understand how such things could happen. Suppose a man does something contrary to one of God's commands. Because divine command theories equate what is commanded by God with what is morally required, such a man does something both morally forbidden and sinful. What he does offends God despite the fact that it does not harm or injure him. God is displeased with the man and looks on him with disfavour unless, perhaps, the man believed with good reason that what he did was not contrary to God's commands. However, if the offence was intentional, God's displeasure seems entirely reasonable, particularly if we may suppose that God's reason for commanding as he did was his love and concern for his creatures. But the man may feel regret for his disobedience later on; he may also form the intention of acting obediently in the future and try to act on this intention. If he does such things, or similar things, then God may respond by renouncing his displeasure and restoring the sinner

[5] Many orthodox theists hold that repentance is a necessary condition of divine forgiveness. See, for example, Wilfred L. Knox, *Penitence and Forgiveness*, London: SPCK (1953). On p. 35, Knox says, 'Penitence is the necessary condition of forgiveness.'

to favour in his eyes. And, if the sinful action has harmed another human, restoration to God's favour may be conditional upon reparations being made, if possible, to the injured party.

So far, I have been narrating the story of divine forgiveness in chronological order. The temporal sequence begins with a divine command being issued. Then someone disobeys the command. At that time or later God becomes displeased with the sinner. Subsequently the sinner repents, and then or later he is restored to God's favour. If repentance involves free action on the part of the sinner and if God has no foreknowledge of free actions, even if he is omniscient, then the temporal sequence is essential to the interaction. If, on the other hand, God does have foreknowledge of the sinner's repentance, the situation is a bit different. God might decide to look on the sinner with disfavour, and make his displeasure apparent to the sinner, knowing all the while that later, when the sinner repents, he will freely give up his negative attitude. Or God might freely decide never to adopt an attitude of disfavour toward the sinner in the light of his knowledge that the sinner will repent later on. If God adopts the second policy, then, even though there is no time when the sinner is looked on with disfavour by God on account of that sin, God would have looked on him with disfavour had he not been going to repent. But God could have done otherwise, and so Minas is mistaken in thinking that, if God forgives us before we petition him to do so, or even before we sin, then this is the only logical possibility open to him and, hence, something with respect to which he cannot make a decision.

I conclude, then, that there is a perfectly sensible interpretation which can be given to the theistic doctrine that God forgives our sins and that, for this reason, there is no conceptual difficulty involved in saying that God has a forgiving disposition or that he sometimes exercises the virtue of forgiveness, though such exercises are not morally required of him as they may be required of us. The doctrine I have been elaborating can be encapsulated in the following definition:

(D5) God forgives the sin x commits in doing A = Df x and A are such that it is sinful that he does it, and he does it, and God would be displeased with him for doing it if he did not repent of doing it, and he does repent of doing it, and there is a time after which God is not displeased with him for doing it.

The third conjunct in the *definiens* is to be understood in such a way that a proposition expressed by a sentence of the form 'God would be displeased with x for doing A if x did not repent of doing A' does not entail either a proposition expressed by a sentence of the form 'For some time t, God is displeased at t with x for doing A' or a proposition expressed by a sentence of the form 'There is no time t such that God is displeased at t with x for doing A'. Thus, (D5) leaves open the question of whether God is ever actually displeased with those sinners who will some day repent. In my opinion, most orthodox theists would hold that God is displeased with sinners who will repent once they have already sinned but not yet repented. However, I see no need to build this feature of what I take to be theistic orthodoxy into a definition of the concept of divine forgiveness. It seems to me, therefore, that I have met the objections Minas raises and vindicated the doctrine that God's activity of forgiving sins consists either in a change of attitude on his part or an act of refraining from adopting a negative attitude.

It is worth noting that contemporary philosophers disagree about whether having been injured or harmed is a necessary condition of exercising forgiveness. R. S. Downie says, 'If A forgives B, then A must have been injured by B: this seems to be a logically necessary condition of forgiveness.'[6] Joseph Beatty holds that the parties in a situation out of which forgiveness can arise are 'an offending person and an offended person'.[7] It is evident that offence and injury are quite different things. I may be offended by someone's bad manners without being injured by them. And I may be injured by someone in a football game without being offended by him. Moreover, it is quite clear that some of the things which theists believe God will forgive are offences but not injuries. The first three commandments of the decalogue specify for Judaeo-Christian theists our main duties to God. Presumably God is offended

[6] R. S. Downie, 'Forgiveness', *Philosophical Quarterly* 15 (1965), pp. 128–34. The quotation is from p. 128.
[7] Joseph Beatty, 'Forgiveness', *American Philosophical Quarterly* 7 (1970), pp. 246–52. The quoted phrase is from p. 247.

if we disobey these commandments but he is not thereby injured in any way. If we disobey these commandments secretly so that no other human being is injured, then such sins are offences but not injuries. I do not claim that such sins as idolatry and blasphemy could never injure other people, but I do maintain that, in so far as they constitute disobedience to God's commands, what God has suffered and may forgive is an offence rather than an injury. And, even in those cases where a sin does injure another human being God is not injured; he is only offended by the disobedient act and has an offence to deal with. Unlike God, we can be both offended and injured and may, therefore, forgive both offences and injuries. Therefore, when we are elaborating a doctrine about God's forgiveness of sins, it seems correct to describe what prompts the negative attitude which God will forswear if he forgives as an offence and not as an injury.

3

I shall now turn my attention to problems concerning the punishment of sins. For analytical purposes, it is useful to distinguish between forgiving a sin and remitting the punishment which is merited by that sin.[8] We may mark this distinction by treating forgiveness and mercy as separate virtues. Obviously we can imagine cases involving human beings where one of these virtues is exercised and the other is not. Thus, for example, suppose that an unlucky thief makes off with a judge's new car and wrecks it before being apprehended. When the thief appears before the judge to be sentenced, he expresses remorse for his deed and promises never to steal again. The judge accepts his display of remorse as genuine and forgives the thief for having injured him. However, knowing that auto theft has been on the increase, he decides to make an example of this thief and hands him a stiff sentence. Here is a case in which the judge exercises forgiveness but not mercy; he forswears his resentment but imposes a stiff punishment none the less. Or,

[8] A parallel distinction is sometimes made in religious writings between removing the barriers to reconciliation with God and full restoration to fellowship with God. Some authors claim that the notion of forgiveness is used in the New Testament to comprehend only the former activity but is used in much recent theology to cover the latter occurrence as well. See, for instance, Vincent Taylor, *Forgiveness and Reconciliation*, London: Macmillan (1952), pp. 2–28.

to vary the example slightly, suppose our unfortunate thief manages to kill his wife and child when he wrecks the judge's car. When he appears to be sentenced, he is grieving but expresses no remorse for having stolen the car. Moreover, the judge was particularly fond of that car. For these reasons, the judge is unable or unwilling to forgive the injury done to him; he continues to resent what the thief has done. But he recognizes that the thief has suffered a great deal in losing his family and so he suspends the thief's sentence. This is a case in which the judge exercises mercy but not forgiveness; his sense of injury persists but he imposes no punishment at all.

When we shift the discussion to the theological level, complications arise. It seems that the punishment of sins, as usually thought of by orthodox theists is primarily retributive. A very powerful deity could, I suppose, arrange the course of nature in such a way that transgressions of his laws were immediately and invariably followed by catastrophic misfortunes. If he did so, it might be reasonable to think of him as punishing in order to deter future transgressions. In this case, if the laws laid down by such a deity were themselves justifiable on utilitarian grounds, then standard utilitarian justifications of punishment could be employed to give a rationale for the way in which our imagined deity governs nature. As far as we can tell, however, the actual course of nature is not a very efficient deterrent against actions of the sort theists typically regard as transgressions against the laws of God. The wicked often prosper while calamities befall the innocent. Moreover, theists suppose that the distribution of punishments and rewards which will rectify things once and for all is to occur in the life of the world to come on the Day of Judgement. But the torments of Hell, or the milder discomforts of Purgatory, are not believed by theists to deter the denizens of those regions from future transgressions. They are retrospective rather than prospective in character. And so, if they have any point or purpose at all, it must be retributive. Those who suffer punishment in the life of the world to come are getting paid back for their past sins.

It is tempting to say that the rewards and punishments meted out on the Day of Judgement are nothing more than God giving to each person what he deserves on the basis of his performance in this life. But we must proceed cautiously here. It is doubtful that all theists would admit that a human being can, strictly speaking, deserve the reward of heavenly bliss. If our fallen state is the source of radical evil in human nature, then perhaps the most that even the best of us could deserve at the hands of God is to be spared the torments of Hell and eventually to take our places in Limbo along with unbaptized infants and virtuous pagans. More seriously, it is open to question whether human beings could have deserts at the hands of God. Theists suppose that God created us, and perhaps a creator may do as he pleases with the things he creates. In Judaeo-Christian religious literature, God is sometimes compared with a potter and we to the clay in his hands.[9] The potter is entitled to do whatever he wishes with his clay; there is nothing the clay can be said to deserve from the potter. If the potter takes a lump of clay and makes from it two jars—a beautiful one for ornament and an ugly one for common use— the ugly jar has no grounds for complaint against the potter because he did not make it beautiful. It is not the case that the potter failed to do for the ugly jar something it deserved. So perhaps no matter how God treats people, here and hereafter, he does not fail to give them what they deserve precisely because there is nothing which creatures can deserve at the hands of their creator. On the other hand, we should not rest too much doctrinal weight on the image of the potter or allow it to mislead us. Theists sometimes compare God to a loving parent, and there is a sense in which parents create their children. But it is quite clear that children do deserve certain sorts of treatment at the hands of their parents, and for this reason we direct moral criticism at parents who mistreat their children. So it may instead be the case that God does parcel out the rewards and punishments of the life of the world to come in accord with our deserts.

Let us see whether we can elaborate a conception of mercy consonant with divine command theories of ethics. Since we

[9] This image appears in the Old Testament in Jeremiah 18:1–6 and in Isaiah 29: 16, for example, and in the New Testament in Romans 9: 20–3. For an interesting discussion of how it is used in Judaism and in Christianity to help deal with some problems about human suffering, see John Bowker, *Problems of Suffering in the Religions of the World*, London: Cambridge University Press (1970), pp. 12–14 and 69–71.

have begun by assuming that mercy involves remission of punishment associated with sin, we must suppose that God somehow ties a certain punishment to each of his commands as the penalty for its violation. Letting the letter 'E' be a variable which ranges over events, we may represent the situation schematically as follows:

(D6) E would be the punishment for x not doing A = Df Person x, action A and event E are such that God commands that the person performs the action, and God stipulates that the event will occur only if the person does not perform the action, and, necessarily, if the event occurs the person suffers.

The system of punishments associated by divine stipulation with failures of obedience to divine commands may be thought of as being as complex as you care to imagine. Punishments might, for example, range from a moment's mild discomfort to an everlasting life of agony and include all degrees of unpleasantness between the two extremes. Nor need we think of the divine stipulations which associate punishments with sins as completely arbitrary. Although God himself is not morally required to command as he does, he may yet have reasons for issuing the commands he does. Perhaps his reasons spring from his love for his creatures and his desire to secure their welfare. If so, he might judge the seriousness of an action contrary to his commands in terms of how much it affects the welfare of his creatures and cleverly match the severity of the punishment to the seriousness of the offence. Finally, it should be noted that the *definiens* does not imply that the punishment will occur if the person does not do what has been commanded; rather it implies that the punishment will occur only if the person does not do what God commands. Hence, the definition leaves open the question of what a sufficient condition for the occurrence of the punishment is. It thereby insures the possibility that God might without altering his stipulation of the connection between offence and punishment bring it about that the punishment does not occur even though the offence has taken place.

We may now define a rather special sense of desert to fit in with the notion of punishment we have already defined. The definition can be stated as follows:

(D7) x deserves the punishment E = Df For some A, E would be
        the punishment for x not doing A and x does not do A.

Hence, a certain person deserves a certain punishment just in
case he disobeys a divine command and God has stipulated
that the punishment occurs only if he disobeys that command.
And, in terms of this notion of desert, we may define successively
the notions of God exercising mercy with respect to a particular
person and a particular punishment and of God exercising
mercy:

(D8) God exercises mercy with respect to the person x who deserves
        the punishment E = Df x deserves the punishment E and
        God brings it about that E does not occur.
(D9) God exercises mercy = Df For some x and some E, God
        exercises mercy with respect to the person x who deserves
        the punishment E.

These definitions express, it seems to me, one intelligible sense
in which a divine command theorist can understand what
would be involved in God's acting mercifully. Of course, if
God does act mercifully, he is not satisfying a moral requirement
in so doing; however, he is sparing one or more of his creatures
some suffering which that creature deserves to undergo. For
this reason, it would seem plausible for us to regard an exercise
of mercy by God as a virtuous act on his part. Several features
of our definitions are worth emphasizing. First, from (D6) we
may infer that, if someone does something commanded by
God, then the event which would be the punishment for that
person not doing that thing will not occur, provided things
happen as God stipulates, as theists believe they must. And so,
since people are punished only when they have disobeyed
divine commands, they are punished only if they violate a
moral requirement. In short, God never punishes the innocent,
no matter what other misfortunes may befall them. Second,
from (D6) and (D7) together, we may infer that a person
deserves a certain punishment only if he has omitted to fulfil a
moral requirement imposed on him by divine command. Thus,
we may say that people deserve punishment from God only
when they fail to live up to the requirements of morality.
Third, according to (D8) and (D9), if God exercises mercy,
then he prevents some event which is the punishment some

person deserves from taking place. We may also say, then, that when God exercises mercy he remits the punishment someone deserves. Fourth, our definitions do not specify a sufficient condition for any punishment to occur; instead they tell us that a necessary part of any sufficient condition for the occurrence of a punishment is that someone has failed to do what God has commanded and what is, therefore, morally required. But it may be, for all we have said, that there are other conditions necessary for the occurrence of punishment. Plausible candidates for such other conditions include such things as an intention not to obey a divine command, a belief that one was not obeying a divine command, a certain freedom of action on the part of the sinner and the like. Moreover, a condition which is surely necessary for such punishment to occur is a free decision by God to allow it to occur or to make it occur, for presumably God has the power to prevent a punishment from occurring even when it is deserved and he is neither obliged nor compelled to allow those who deserve punishment to suffer it. Fifth, our definitions provide no sufficient conditions for any exercise of God's mercy other than his remission of a deserved punishment; rather they tell us that prevention of suffering by God would be an exercise of mercy by God just in case the suffering in question were also a deserved punishment. And perhaps there are conditions other than someone's deserving punishment which must be satisfied before God will ever exercise mercy by preventing suffering. Candidates are such things as repentance on the part of the sinner, feelings of remorse, attempts at reparations to those harmed by the sin if feasible, and so forth. However, for all our definitions say explicitly, God may exercise mercy with respect to persons who deserve punishment at his pleasure. This is as things should be within the framework of divine command theories. God has no moral obligation to exercise mercy if such other conditions are satisfied; he has no moral duty to prevent punishments which are deserved from taking place. But God also has no obligation to refrain from exercising mercy unless such further conditions are satisfied; he has no moral duty to allow sinners to suffer the punishments they deserve if they do not repent. Whether or not God exercises mercy is, as far as our definitions go, up to him to decide as he pleases, and whether or not he allows or causes sinners who deserve punishment to suffer their punishment is also, according to our definitions, something for him to decide at his pleasure.

Although we have defined the notion of deserving punishment, we have not defined the notion of deserving mercy. And we should now ask ourselves whether a human being can deserve mercy from God. If we look closely at this issue we seem to confront a dilemma. On the one hand, if we assume that a person can deserve mercy from God and that justice is giving people what they deserve, then mercy would be required by justice. But then what are we to make of the admonition that justice should be tempered with mercy? On the other hand, if we assume that people cannot deserve mercy from God and that God has no obligation or duty to exercise mercy, then even if God does not exercise mercy he is not subject to moral condemnation for being merciless. But would we not agree that if God does not show mercy to the repentant sinner he is morally blameworthy?[10] From the standpoint of divine command theories, it is clear that the first horn of the dilemma should be rejected and that the second should be accepted. We must reject the first horn because, according to divine command theories, nothing is morally required of God. We must say instead that either people cannot deserve mercy from God or divine justice does not consist in giving people exactly what they deserve. We can admit that divine justice is giving people exactly what they deserve so long as we bear in mind that nothing imposes a moral requirement on God to act justly. If God does give people exactly what they deserve and thereby exercises justice, he does so without being required to do so. And we can also deny that people ever deserve mercy from God. People who fail to obey his commands deserve punishment, and if they are spared punishment, then they have been treated by God better than they deserve to be. Confronting God, we may hope that he will temper justice with mercy when we have sinned and deserve punishment, and since God loves us this hope has some foundation in the nature of things.

---

[10] This formulation is adapted from a puzzle about human justice and human mercy stated by James P. Sterba in 'Can a Person Deserve Mercy?', a paper read at the Western Division Meeting of the American Philosophical Association in 1976.

But we would not be entitled to complain against God if he failed to temper justice with mercy, for he would then be giving people exactly what they deserve. We must accept the second horn because, according to divine command theory, God is not subject to moral condemnation no matter what he does. We must say that God has no duty or obligation to exercise mercy, even when he is dealing with a repentant sinner, and so he is not morally blameworthy if he does not do so. If God does show mercy to the repentant sinner, to the person who sins unintentionally and to similar people of good will, then he is gracious in doing so. And, if God loves us, we have reason to hope that he will act graciously toward such people, and possibly toward others as well. I believe that many Judaeo-Christian theists hold that God does exercise mercy toward repentant sinners, and perhaps others, but that he always acts graciously when he does this precisely because such people do not deserve mercy. For this reason, I am inclined to think that a divine command theory should not rule out the possibility that people who fail to obey God's commands deserve punishment but do not deserve mercy even if they repent. Lest this asymmetry seem disturbing, it should be added that people who do not fail to obey God's commands do not deserve punishment. Of course, they may not deserve rewards either, for such rewards as God gives may also always be bestowed graciously. We might describe God's acts of mercy as supererogatory provided we understand a supererogatory divine act to be one which God wishes to have done, and so chooses to do, without being required to do it or commanding himself to do it.

We will, I suggest, be in a position to avoid certain confusions if we bear in mind that the technical conceptions of desert and mercy which I have contrived to fit smoothly into a divine command conception of God's attributes are rather different from those appropriate to the discussion of ordinary human moral and legal affairs. Consider, for example, the view advanced by Alwynne Smart, according to which there are two main conceptions of mercy. As the first conception has it, acts of mercy are measures by which we try to ensure that the punishment really fits the crime by avoiding unduly harsh penalties which an inflexible legal system might otherwise impose upon an offender. According to the second conception, we exercise mercy when we benevolently impose less than the deserved punishment on an offender in cases where such leniency is dictated by the claims other obligations have on us.[11] Obviously a divine command theorist will hold that God exercises mercy in neither of these ways. On the one hand, God's system of moral requirements and associated punishments can be as flexible as it needs to be in order to treat each case on its own merits; in addition, the punishment fits the crime by definition in God's system since it is God who defines what the crimes are, and stipulates, perhaps for good reasons, what punishment is to be associated with each. And even a theist who does not accept a divine command theory can claim that, because God is both omniscient and omnipotent, the punishment always fits the crime like a glove in God's moral system. On the other hand, God could not, for a divine command theorist, benevolently impose less than the deserved punishment because of the claims other obligations have on him. There are no obligations which have claims on God, and so if he benevolently imposes less than the deserved punishment it must be for other reasons than the claims of obligation. Moreover, it is doubtful whether theists who reject divine command theories would find Smart's second conception an acceptable account of divine mercy. They might maintain that the deserved punishment is the one which God ought to impose on the sinner in the light of all the obligations which have claims upon him.

Similarly, the rather subtle attempt by Claudia Card to justify a principle setting forth the desert bases of a case for mercy makes use of a conception of mercy different from the one which I have argued is appropriate for use with reference to God as thought of by the divine command theorist. The principle Card advocates goes as follows: 'Mercy ought to be shown to an offender when it is evident that otherwise (1) he would be made to suffer unusually more on the whole, owing to his peculiar misfortunes, than he deserves in view of his basic character and (2) he would be worse off in this respect than those who stand to benefit from the exercise of their right to

---

[11] Alwynne Smart, 'Mercy', *Philosophy* 43 (1968), pp. 345–59. See especially pp. 353–8.

punish him (or to have him punished).'[12] According to Card, when the conditions of this principle are met, the offender deserves mercy, although desert of mercy does not give rise to an obligation. There are, I believe, at least four reasons for doubting that this principle sets forth the desert bases for a case of divine mercy. First, it may be that exercises of divine mercy are not based on desert at all. If we are all corrupted owing to the presence of radical evil in human nature, then it may be that we deserve punishment but never mercy. At any rate, as we have defined things, an exercise of divine mercy does not entail that the person to whom mercy is shown deserves to be treated mercifully. Second, even if human beings can deserve things from God, the basis of any case for divine mercy may well be quite different from anything expressed by Card's principle. If, for example, repentance and remorse by the sinner are necessary conditions for deserving divine mercy, as some theists believe, then repentance and remorse are necessary parts of any sufficient condition of deserving divine mercy. If so, then Card's principle does not express a sufficient condition of deserving divine mercy. Third, it may be that condition (1) in Card's principle is never satisfied when it is a question of what we deserve from God in view of our basic character. If, as the theological doctrine of original sin implies, our basic characters are all such that we deserve only everlasting damnation from God, then no matter what a person's peculiar misfortunes may be, he will not suffer more than he deserves in view of his basic character. Should this be the case, Card's principle does not provide a desert basis of a case for divine mercy when and if divine mercy is deserved. Finally, it may be that condition (2) in Card's principle is never satisfied when it is a question of God punishing a sinner. When God allows a sinner to be punished or punishes him, he does not benefit from having him punished or punishing him, and there is no one else who has the right to execute the punishments reserved to God. Thus, no matter how badly off a divinely punished sinner might be, he would not be worse off than anyone who both stands to benefit from his being punished and

---

[12] Claudia Card, 'On Mercy', *Philosophical Review* 81 (1972), pp. 182–207. The principle I have quoted is stated on p. 184.

exercises a right to punish him or to have him punished. Since this is the case, Card's principle does not provide a desert basis of a case for divine mercy. We may, therefore, safely conclude that Card's conception of the relation between human desert and human mercy is different from a conception which would be adequate to a divine command theorist's notion of the relation, if any, between human desert and divine mercy.

This is, of course, not to say that Smart and Card fail to analyse important features of the conception of mercy which is suitable for use in discussing retribution within human social institutions and moral practices. All I claim to have shown is that their views are not adequate to the notion of divine mercy, particularly as that notion is to be understood in the context of divine command theories. In short, the human moral virtue of mercy and the divine character trait of mercifulness are different things, and the two virtues are appropriately exercised under different circumstances. This conclusion should come as no surprise to anyone who has followed the argument thus far, but confusion will be avoided if it is kept firmly in mind.

4

Theists of all stripes would insist that God is perfectly just. But divine command theorists will hasten to add that God's justice does not consist in conformity to a standard of action independent of his will. God, they will say, has no duty to be just; he is under no moral obligation to exercise the virtue of justice. Moreover, many theists hold that God sometimes exercises the virtue of mercy and spares sinners from undergoing the punishments they deserve. Indeed, if we are all corrupted by original sin, then anyone who is spared punishment is the beneficiary of an act of divine mercy. But how is it possible for a just God to spare sinners from undergoing the punishments they deserve?

Anselm saw that there are some philosophical puzzles about how justice and mercy can both be attributes of God, and he wrestles with a few related problems of this sort in the *Proslogium*. The first problem is stated in this fashion:

Or, what justice is that to give him who merits eternal death everlasting life? How, then, gracious Lord, good to the righteous and the wicked, canst thou save the wicked if this is not just, and thou dost not aught that is not just?[13]

Clearly what is at issue in this passage is a kind of retributive justice on the part of God. The assumption which underlies the questions seems to be that retributive justice consists in giving people exactly what they deserve. Since the wicked deserve to be punished, it would be just for God to punish them. If God then spares the wicked and remits their deserved punishment, he does not act justly. Either God acts justly and treats the wicked as they deserve by punishing them, or God spares the wicked some punishment they have deserved and does not act justly. Hence, either God is just but not merciful or he is merciful but not just. A simple solution to this problem can be fabricated; one only needs to change the underlying assumption a bit. Instead of supposing that retributive justice consists in treating people exactly as they deserve, we might assume that retributive justice consists only in treating people no worse than they deserve. Thus, God does no injustice to the sinners he punishes because he treats them no worse than they deserve, but he does no injustice to the sinners he spares because he treats them no worse, and in fact a great deal better, than they deserve. If this were all that needs to be said about the matter, then it would be easy to see how God could be both just and merciful in exacting retribution from sinners.

However, a system of retribution is just only if it is fair, which is to say, only if it treats relevantly similar cases in the same manner. Morally speaking, the relevant respect of similarity among sinners according to divine command theories is that they have all failed to obey a divine command and thereby come to deserve punishment. Hence, a just God would treat all sinners alike; either he would punish each as that sinner deserves or he would spare all and punish none. Or, at least, so it seems. The real problem is not how God can spare the wicked who deserve punishment. He can do this easily enough by leaving Hell, Purgatory, and other such unsavoury niches in the divine ecology unoccupied. Instead, the problem

---

[13] Anselm, *Basic Writings* (tr. S. N. Deane), LaSalle: Open Court (1962), p. 14. The quoted passage is from *Proslogium* IX.

is how a just God can spare some of the wicked and punish others, as many theists believe God in fact does.

And Anselm offers no satisfactory solution to this problem. One thing he says about it is this:

> For, he who is good, both to the righteous and the wicked, is better than he who is good to the good alone; and he who is good to the wicked, both by punishing and sparing them, is better than he who is good by punishing them alone.[14]

It may be that God would be perfectly fair if he were to spare both the righteous and the wicked as well as if he were to spare the righteous and to punish the wicked. But it seems evident that God would not be perfectly fair if he chose to punish some of the wicked and to spare others. And so it seems clear that God would not be just if he spared some of the wicked and punished others, unless there is some good reason for distinguishing between those among the wicked who are to be punished and those who are to be spared. Thus, Anselm can derive no aid from the following recourse to divine command theory:

> For, it is not just that those whom thou dost will to punish should be saved, and that those whom thou dost will to spare should be condemned. For that alone is just which thou dost will; and that alone unjust which thou dost not will.[15]

The divine command theorist will acknowledge that what God wills or commands determines what is morally required. What moral justice requires of us depends on what God wills, and God cannot be condemned for acting in a way which is morally unjust if he spares some wicked people and punishes others. But unless there is some reason for a distinction between those he punishes and those he spares, he acts unfairly when he arbitrarily spares some and punishes others. And, if he acts unfairly, then he is not perfectly just. Thus, even though divine justice is not a moral virtue, still it is an attribute which God would lack if he were to discriminate arbitrarily in choosing to spare some of the wicked and to punish others. Therefore, if God does so discriminate when he exercises

---

[14] Ibid., pp. 14–15. The quoted passage is from *Proslogium* IX.
[15] Ibid., p. 18. The quoted passage is from *Proslogium* XI.

mercy, then he does not act justly in the matter of retributive punishments.

Someone who wishes to hold that God is perfectly just even though he mercifully spares some sinners and punishes others as they deserve can, of course, claim that there is, unknown to us and perhaps unknowable by us, some reason for this apparently invidious discriminatory behaviour. This view seems to represent Anselm's final word on the subject:

> But if it can be comprehended in any way why thou canst will to save the wicked, yet by no consideration can we comprehend why, of those who are alike wicked, thou savest some rather than others, through supreme goodness; and why thou dost condemn the latter rather than the former, through supreme justice.[16]

It may be that we cannot comprehend why God punishes some of the wicked and spares others but that there is, none the less, a reason why God acts as he does in these matters. After all, some of the theistic religions are taken by their adherents to contain many incomprehensible mysteries, and this could easily be one of them. As long as we do not comprehend this, however, the possibility remains open that there is no reason why God punishes some of the wicked and spares others; and so it remains possible, for all we know, that God acts arbitrarily and unfairly when he exercises mercy in some cases rather than others. If this were the case, God would not always act justly in dealing out retribution. It is, therefore, a matter of some urgency to find, if we can, a basis for divine discriminations in the treatment of sinners.

We can, I think, define a slightly different notion of desert which will provide a solution to our problem based on desert of mercy. Starting from (D6), we adopt instead of (D7) the following pair of definitions:

(D10) x merits the punishment E for not having done A = Df E would be the punishment for x not doing A and x does not do A.

(D11) x deserves the punishment E = Df For some A, x merits the punishment E for not having done A and x does not repent of not having done A.

16 The Ibid., pp. 18–19. quoted passage is from *Proslogium* XI.

According to our new definitions, someone deserves a certain punishment just in case he has failed to obey a divine command to which that punishment is attached and has also failed to repent of his failure to obey. Next we may define a concept of deserving the remission of a merited punishment in the following way:

(D12) x deserves the remission of punishment E = Df For some A, x merits the punishment E for not having done A and x repents of not having done A.

Hence, someone deserves the remission of a certain punishment just in case he has failed to obey a divine command to which that punishment is attached but has repented of his failure to obey. Next we need to redefine the notion of divine mercy. This can be done in the following way:

(D13) God exercises mercy with respect to the person x who merits the punishment E = Df For some A, x merits the punishment E for not having done A and God brings it about that E does not occur.

(D14) God exercises mercy = Df For some x and some E, God exercises mercy with respect to the person x who merits the punishment E.

Taken together, (D13) and (D14) imply that God exercises the virtue of mercy just in case he prevents some merited punishment from occurring. However, they do not imply that God exercises mercy only by preventing punishments whose remission is deserved or that he never exercises mercy by preventing punishments which are deserved. For all that these definitions tell us, God might mercifully prevent all merited punishments, or some which are deserved and some whose remission is deserved, or only those whose remission is deserved. Finally, we require definitions which will capture the notion of divine retributive justice. Such definitions may be formulated in the following way:

(D15) God exercises justice with respect to the person x who merits the punishment E = Df Either x deserves the punishment E and God brings it about that E occurs, or x deserves the remission of punishment E and God brings it about that E does not occur.

(D16) God exercises justice $=$ Df For some x and some E, God exercises justice with respect to the person x who merits the punishment E.

According to (D15) and (D16), whenever God exercises justice, people get what they deserve. If they deserve punishment, God brings it about that their punishment occurs; if they deserve the remission of merited punishment, he brings it about that their punishment does not occur. Hence, if God never fails to exercise justice when the opportunity arises, he only exercises mercy toward those persons whose punishment is merited but not deserved and he exercises mercy toward all such persons. We may, then, give a relatively precise account of the reasons for which God with perfect justice spares some sinners and punishes others. He mercifully spares all and only those sinners who repent. Because their merited punishment deserves to be remitted, he gives them what they deserve and so acts justly in exercising his mercy toward them. He punishes all and only those sinners who do not repent. Because their merited punishment is deserved, he gives them what they deserve too and so acts justly in not exercising his mercy toward them. In either case, God does not fail to act justly. Moreover, since repentance seems a fair basis for discriminating among sinners, in treating repentant sinners and unrepentant sinners differently God does not act unfairly when he acts mercifully toward all the members of one group but does not act mercifully toward any member of the other.

Some theists may wish to hold that there are conditions other than repentance for having sinned which could contribute to desert of remission. Examples are absence of an intention to disobey God, excusably mistaken beliefs about what God has commanded, infirmities beyond the control of the agent which make it psychologically or physically impossible to do what has been commanded and similar conditions which might plausibly be taken to count as excuses for disobedience to God. Such conditions can be accommodated easily enough within our framework. We only need to modify (D12) so that its second conjunct is a disjunction of all those conditions such that our theist believes that satisfaction of one or more of them creates desert of remission; then we must also alter (D11) so that its second conjunct is the negation of that disjunction. Hence, it is not an objection to the general strategy embodied in (D10)–(D16) that it over-simplifies the reasons which justify in God's eyes the remission of merited punishment. No matter how complicated those conditions may actually turn out to be, they can without difficulty be incorporated into definitions which are close analogues of (D11) and (D12).

Some theists hold the view that, strictly speaking, no one could deserve the remission of punishment merited by sin because they hold that in exercising mercy God acts graciously and treats sinners better than they deserve to be treated. This view too can be worked out rather neatly with only minor modifications in the system of ideas we have been elaborating. First, we replace (D11) with a somewhat simpler definition:

(D17) x deserves the punishment E = Df For some A, x merits the punishment E for not having done A.

Then we substitute for (D12) this definition:

(D18) God has reasons for remitting the punishment E which x merits = Df For some A, x merits the punishment E for not having done A and x repents of not having done A.

And, if there are reasons for divine remission of merited punishment other than repentance, an analogue of (D18) whose second conjunct is a disjunction whose disjuncts enumerate all and only the reasons for such remission can be formulated to take care of them. Finally, we replace (D15) with the following definition:

(D19) God exercises justice with respect to the person x who merits the punishment E = Df Either x deserves the punishment E and God does not have reasons for remitting the punishment E which x merits and God brings it about the E occurs, or x deserves the punishment E and God has reasons for remitting the punishment E which x merits and God brings it about that E does not occur.

According to our latest definitions, whenever someone disobeys a divine command, that person deserves the associated punishment. Hence, even if God has reasons for remitting a punishment which someone merits, that person deserves the punishment in question. But God acts justly in punishing and sparing just in case he treats those who deserve punishment no worse than they deserve. On the one hand, if someone deserves a certain punishment and God has no reasons for remitting it, then God acts justly in punishing that sinner because God treats him exactly as he deserves to be treated. On the other hand, if someone deserves a certain punishment and God has reasons for remitting it, then God acts justly in mercifully sparing that sinner because for certain reasons God treats him better than he deserves to be treated. Therefore, if God is perfectly just, he exercises mercy toward all and only those sinners who are such that he has reasons for remitting their deserved punishments, and he does not exercise mercy toward those sinners who are such that he has no reason for remitting their deserved punishment but punishes them instead. If God acted in this way, he would not act unfairly. Those who were punished would have no grounds for complaint against God because they would have been treated exactly as they deserve. Moreover, they would have no grounds for envy of those who had been mercifully spared because there would be such factors as repentance to serve as God's reasons for sparing such people. And, of course, those who were spared should be grateful to God for having graciously treated them better than they deserved.

It seems to me that the sequence of definitions consisting of (D6), (D10), (D17), a somewhat more complex version of (D18), (D13), (D14), (D19), and (D16) expresses a doctrine which captures the principal features of the theory of retribution most congenial to the mainstream of Judaeo-Christian orthodoxy. If this is correct, then we have succeeded in solving Anselm's problems about the relation between divine justice and divine mercy in a fashion compatible with both a divine command theory of ethics and a major strand of theistic orthodoxy. God can be perfectly just while punishing some of the wicked who deserve to be punished and mercifully sparing others who deserve punishment no less but who do such things as repenting which provide God with reasons for remitting their punishment. God's justice and mercy are not, according to divine command theories, moral virtues because, strictly speaking, God has no duty or obligation to cultivate or exercise them. Nevertheless, they are similar enough to the analogous human moral virtues that it is not a bit misleading to call both members of each pair by the same name. And these divine attributes are excellences of a certain sort, ones which it would be fitting for a being worthy of worship and obedience to possess.

5

I conclude that, at least with respect to the issues we have examined, the charge that divine command theories of ethics are not acceptable for theological reasons has been refuted. We have seen that a loving God who is such that what is morally required is necessarily coextensive with what he commands can possess and exercise such character traits as a forgiving spirit, mercy, and justice. Though God is not morally required to have, to cultivate or to exercise such dispositions as these, there is no problem of logical coherence in attributing each of them or all of them to God. Moreover, they all seem to be character traits which a being who loves and commands us as a good parent would do, who merits both our obedience and our devotion, ought to possess. Thus, there seems to be no good reason for supposing that divine command theories cannot be used to good effect in giving a theologically illuminating account of the nature of God. Such an account, if it is of the sort I have been engaged in constructing, also appears to be philosophically respectable. Moreover, I would also say that divine command theorists are entitled to hope at least, and perhaps also to believe if they wish, that there is a being who has the excellences of character which theists usually attribute to God, or very similar attributes, and who is the author of the human moral law.

Index